Learn Science, Learn Math,
Learn to Teach Science and Math,
Homo Sapiens!

CULTURAL PERSPECTIVES IN SCIENCE EDUCATION: RESEARCH DIALOGS

Volume No 5

Series Editor

Kenneth Tobin, *The Graduate Center, City University of New York, USA*

Catherine Milne, *Steinhardt School of Culture, Education , and Human Development, New York University*

Scope

Research dialogs consists of books written for undergraduate and graduate students of science education, teachers, parents, policy makers, and the public at large. Research dialogs bridge theory, research, and the practice of science education. Books in the series focus on what we know about key topics in science education – including, teaching, connecting the learning of science to the culture of students, emotions and the learning of science, labs, field trips, involving parents, science and everyday life, scientific literacy, including the latest technologies to facilitate science learning, expanding the roles of students, after school programs, museums and science, doing dissections, etc.

LEARN SCIENCE, LEARN MATH, LEARN TO TEACH SCIENCE AND MATH, *HOMO SAPIENS!*

HEDY MOSCOVICI

ILLUSTRATIONS BY TAL MOSCOVICI

CHAPTER 6, BY
KATHERINE C. WIESEMAN AND HEDY MOSCOVICI

FINAL EDITING BY
PENNY J. GILMER AND KATHERINE C. WIESEMAN

SENSE PUBLISHERS
ROTTERDAM / TAIPEI

A C.I.P. record for this book is available from the Library of Congress.

ISBN: 978-94-6209-153-5 (Paperback)
ISBN: 978-94-6209-154-2 (Hardback)
ISBN: 978-94-6209-155-9 (e-book)

Published by: Sense Publishers,
P.O. Box 21858,
3001 AW Rotterdam,
The Netherlands
https://www.sensepublishers.com/

Printed on acid-free paper

TABLE OF CONTENTS

ILLUSTRATIONS

DEDICATION

Hold fast to dreams
For if dreams die
Life is a broken-winged bird
That cannot fly.
Hold fast to dreams
For when dreams go
Life is a barren field
Frozen with snow.
("Dreams," Hughes, 2012)

Reading this poem, which was in an email from a dear colleague and friend
in the last week of my life, and deeply breathing the aroma from a fragrant
rose, given to me by a nurse at Torrance Memorial Hospital,
helped me remember what matters.

ACKNOWLEDGMENTS

My husband, Uri, and three sons, Danny, Tal, and Ido, for their steadfast love through all the years especially the last 5-½.

Educators, friends, and family, especially my parents and family in Romania and Israel, who encouraged and supported me from the day I was born to become and be the person I am.

Penny J. Gilmer, Professor Emerita of Chemistry and Biochemistry, Florida State University, and Katherine C. Wieseman, Educational Consultant, for completing the book and taking it to publication.

Tal Moscovici for creating the cartoons and illustrations.

Leni (Lenora) Cook, Professor Emerita in English, California State University-Dominguez Hills, and Janet Dubinsky, Medical School Professor, University of Minnesota-Minneapolis, who reviewed some of the chapters.

Peter de Liefde, founder and manager of Sense Publishing, for his compassion and generosity in extending deadlines so the book could be finished.

Ken Tobin, Presidential Professor of Urban Studies, The Graduate Center, City University of New York, for finding the publisher of this book and for being a constant mentor and a friend, beginning when I became a doctoral student at Florida State University.

The editors thank Lily Navon, a friend of Hedy's, for reading Hedy's book and making suggestions for clarifications in a close to final version of the text.

ABBREVIATIONS

Advanced Placement	AP
American Association for the Advancement of Science	AAAS
The Association for Science Teacher Education	ASTE
Functional Magnetic Resonance Imaging	fMRI
Fluency in Instructional Technology	FITness
Grade Point Average	GPA
Information and Communication Technology	ICT
Information Technology	IT
Los Angeles United School District	LAUSD
NARST—A Worldwide Organization for Improving Science Teaching and	
Learning Through Research	NARST
National Council of Teachers of Mathematics	NCTM
National Science Teachers Association	NSTA
National Research Council	NRC
National Science Education Standards	NSES
No Child Left Behind	NCLB
Pedagogical Content Knowledge	PCK
Programme for International Student Assessment	PISA
Quality Educator Development	QED
Scholastic Aptitude Test	SAT
Standardized Testing and Reporting	STAR
System-wide Change of All Learners and Educators	SCALE
Trends in International Mathematics and Science Study	TIMSS
United States of America	USA

FOREWORD

When we walk in the sand on a beach, we leave footprints that others may notice (at least until the next wave or tide washes over and erases them). No longer can we walk on the beach alongside and talk with Dr. Hedy Moscovici about her unique worldview and perspective of science and mathematics learning and teaching. All we can do is study a footprint trail, which she leaves in the form of this, her first and only book, in which she bids us adieu with a statement about her most important learning - "...I have learned that above all, 'love is the most positive energy we have'" (Orloff, 2005, p. 157) - and the essential question is – "in the end, what really matters to you to Learn Science, Learn Math, Learn To Teach Science and Mathematics, *Homo sapiens*?" (Moscovici, 2012;. 116).

Hedy was a woman, science and mathematics educator, researcher, colleague, friend, daughter, mother, and wife who lived her 56 years on three continents. She was born and spent her childhood and teenage years in socialist Romania (in Eastern Europe); she spent her young adult years in Israel (in Southwestern Asia); she moved to the United States (in North America), for her doctoral studies at Florida State University and lived her professional life in the states of Washington and California until her untimely death in November 2011. These experiences helped her develop her persona, as a science and mathematics teacher and learner, and facilitated the formation of her worldview, as symbolized by the tripartite flag (Figure F. 1).

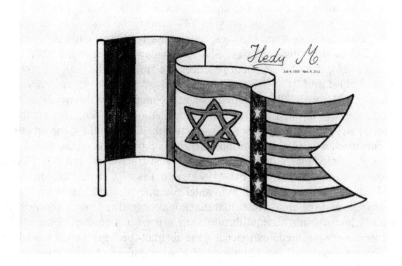

Figure F.1. Flag from Hedy Moscovici's office at California State University-Dominguez Hills, representing her having lived in three countries.

Hedy's flag above summarizes a tripartite theme evident in her worldview, in stories she shared about her life, in key messages communicated in this book, and in the universal questions she raises throughout the book – Whom, for what reason, and why are we educating? These universal questions are ones posed by diverse audiences who care about schooling. These audiences include prospective and practicing teachers wanting to motivate their students to learn, science and mathematics educators mentoring teachers to become transformative intellectuals and critical pedagogues, parents interested in their children's advancement, and interested policymakers and public wishing to deepen their understanding about learning in general and educational issues in science and mathematics.

In chapter 1 we meet Hedy, a young girl living in socialist Romania. She juggles her desires for play and friendship, responsibilities as a family member, and drive for academic success in a school system that did not differentiate expectations according to gender or socioeconomic status. As we read, we piece together a tripartite theme - human ability for and necessity of thinking (because we are cognizing beings), pervasiveness of emotion in all aspects of living and learning (because we are also emotional beings), and influential interplay of factors such as socioeconomic profile, political context, gender, race, and expectations from family and school personnel (because we are members in the communities in which we experience life). Using worldview as a theoretical framework, Hedy's stories about her years as a student in Romania, Israel, and the United States illustrate the significance of "bumps" or disequilibria as necessary ingredients for growth, development and change. She makes explicit ways in which established norms, political events such as war, and cultural values such as family's sense of togetherness, are part of the invisible matrix of disequilibrium in learning and interpreting of life experiences. The chapter ends with the spotlight on the need to educate today's students for citizenry in 21st century communities, which, as a result of global challenges and changes, requires skills dramatically different from skills needed in previous centuries. She foreshadows the criticism that current curricula, pedagogy, and assessment practices are "missing the mark" - and are in drastic need of reform.

In chapter 2 Hedy unveils a detailed look at the meaning of the words to "learn" and "understand" - through a constructivist epistemological lens formed from an amalgam of several dimensions of constructivism: Glasersfeld's construction of radical constructivism (1991b); various theorists' explications of the social aspect of learning, including Vygotskian's social constructivism (1978); Cobern's contextual or cultural constructivism (1993); and Taylor's critical constructivism. (1996). Hedy reminds us that each individual's journey to think, know and become wise is unique, and she emphasizes that maximum cognitive growth depends on an individual's journey into disequilibrium with a perfect blending of the concrete (often a tactile or kinesthetic experience), the abstract (perhaps mental modeling or passive observation) and the emotional (feelings associated with cognitive and physical activity).

Complementary to the aforementioned trifold theme on the nature of learning is another trifold theme. This theme gives attention to the affective realm, namely the importance of interweaving *respect* (teacher-student as well as student-student), *rights* (students' and teachers' rights to ask questions), and *responsibility* (a teacher's responsibility to challenge students and students' responsibility to challenge themselves). She presents a dilemma related to measurement of learning - we live in a society in which objective and accurate measurement of quality is deeply valued, yet no clearly trustworthy "learning meter" exists. School systems worldwide use various tools to assess, evaluate, and grade students' knowledge as well as the quality of teaching, and she questions the health of the connection between assessment and teaching methodologies.

Reading chapter 3 may trigger a reader's "bellyache" and an "emotional cascade" as the brain navigates the cognitively demanding and emotionally arousing descriptions of neuroscience research, whose ultimate purpose is an explanation of emotion-cognition interactions and affective-cognitive structures in the context of learning, particularly learning in school classrooms. Hedy's Chapter 3 provides a study of the magical, mysterious, and not completely understood triadic interaction of emotion, rational thought/cognition, and physical body processes. In this chapter about the neurobiology and neurochemistry of emotions, we learn about the tricky balance between negative emotions or energy (pain) and positive emotions or energy (pleasure), which shape cognitive endeavors and influence Csikszentmihalyi's "flow channel" for successful learning. We cannot ignore the pervasive presence of emotion (e.g., anxiety, fear, shame, disappointment, confusion, boredom, happiness, enjoyment) in life and learning experiences in Hedy's childhood stories about playing games (i.e., Sus-Jos, Tarile), and completing and presenting school assignments (e.g., written composition). Hedy raises her concern about an often-implied "not understanding science [and math] gene," which she thinks is creating a new sociocultural norm and attributed to be an origin for science and mathematics phobias in US culture. She ends this chapter by promoting Orloff's idea of emotions associated with positive energy, with an emphasis on pleasure, as the matrix for the affective domain in school classrooms in order to encourage learners' buy-in for learning.

In Chapter 4, Hedy's mottos, "I cannot learn from you if you cannot learn from me," and "to teach is to learn twice," blossom with the ideas that learning science and mathematics and learning to teach are lifelong processes. As a critical pedagogue with a heightened awareness of power relationships in the classroom, Hedy advocates nurturing respectful co-learning, collaboration, and cooperation. Hedy characterizes this classroom culture by 1) teachers promoting a triad of inquiry, problem-solving and critical thinking in the cognitive realm; 2) students' internal compasses consistently pointing in a direction comprised of three sub-aspects, namely positive emotion, positive self-efficacy, and conceptual understanding; and 3) flow of learning which underscores interconnection and the personal, rather than the disconnected and impersonal; provides scaffolding between the abstract and concrete; and, maximizes pleasure rather than pain. In her worldview, learning to teach involves becoming a transformative intellectual with pedagogical content knowledge. The stories she shares feature different dimensions of her journey to become such a teacher. She allows us to view her, troubled and vulnerable, as she struggles to understand ways to bring pleasure into her students' learning experiences when it is obvious that her passion and pleasure are not mirrored in their emotional experiences.

Chapter 5 responds to a question which Hedy poses in the chapter's opening, "How does one lead in a [changing] world in which information is readily available and technology is becoming more and more affordable and innovative?" The essence of the answer can be found in the idea that leading, like learning, is a partner relationship – in short, co-leadership fashioned from a blend of aspects of egalitarian leadership, participative leadership, and mindful attention to rights and responsibilities. The choice of leader depends on what one knows and is expert about, and what is needed in the situation. On the vastness of literature on the leadership topic, Hedy considers that she only uses the tip of an iceberg. We suggest that the reader might expand this viewpoint by pondering the metaphor as a model, akin to Kohls' (1990) conceptualization of an iceberg model of culture.

In chapter 6 Hedy showers us with everyday life events from her life as a mother of three boys. These everyday events invite us to think of scientific and mathematical knowledge as tools for making sense of and engaging in the world as well as the communities in which we (hopefully as informed consumers) live. They also open us to consider myriad possibilities of which we might not otherwise be aware — providing evidence of discipline-specific and interdependent concepts and principles in action, and demonstrate cognition-emotion connections.

For us (Katherine and Penny), the story in chapter 6 evoking the greatest disequilibrium is the one revealing her viewpoint on the ultimate challenge for human existence. Regardless whether we (and she) intellectually understand and can explain the interconnectedness of cognition-emotion, her experience with (and death as a result of) ovarian cancer presents us with this undeniable connection – an experience of and journey into exploring pain, for her and likely too for many readers.

Emotion is present in every learning experience, whether the experience is in a school classroom or in daily life, and somehow emotion mediates the learning that happens. The question of what matters most in teaching and learning science and mathematics might best be answered with two phrases: emotional connection... human relationships. Teachers and students somehow need to connect emotionally with each other. A teacher can initiate a journey of relationship and student participation in learning by knowing and recognizing the student as a human with assets (strengths and expertise) and by promoting positive energy (emotions) in the classroom. The student can acknowledge this invitation and further the relationship by connecting with the material being learned and other humans in her life.

Katherine C. Wieseman, Ph.D.
Penny J. Gilmer, Ph.D., D. Sc.Ed.

WORLDVIEW AS A DYNAMIC ENTITY

THE EVOLVING ME

I have lived my life on three continents – childhood and teen-age years in Socialist Romania (Eastern Europe), young adulthood in Israel (Southwestern Asia), and mature adulthood to the present in the United States of America (USA in North America). Experiences in these different countries and their set sequence helped me become the science and mathematics learner and teacher that I am today and informed my worldviews. While this book focuses on successful learning and teaching of science and mathematics, I need to acknowledge the fact that the different systems and contexts have molded my views on other issues too (e.g., education, family, heterogeneous populations, roles for females and males in society, government systems, role of language, place of religion in life, meaning of birthplace, armed services, and human need to make choices as well as the role and attitude toward imposed rules and regulations).

As mentioned in the chapter title, I conceptualize my worldview as changing relatively slowly because of political and social changes through time (e.g., movement of Romania from socialism to democracy after Ceausescu's death), or more dramatically by my moving to other countries, and/or being introduced and asked to reflect on others' worldviews. In my personal case, I consider emigrating from Romania to Israel in 1973 and later arriving in the USA to study for my PhD in 1991 as leading to dramatic changes in my worldview.

For this book, I focus on the slice of my worldview related to schooling, and more precisely to learning and teaching science and mathematics. I share its dynamics in retrospect.

All the themes, like schooling, community, stratification, gender and race, as well as issues related to leadership and government, were a vital part of my life as a child in socialist Romania. I continue these themes when I describe my perspective on schooling and society in Israel where, at the Hebrew University in Jerusalem I studied for a bachelor's degree in Biology/General Science, a master's degree in Parasitology, and the credential programs for secondary science and mathematics teaching; and worked as a research associate and research laboratory manager for a researcher in the Parasitology Department. My career continued with science and mathematics teaching for six years in secondary schools in Israel.

My arrival in the USA to pursue a Ph.D. in Science Education represents a dramatic change in the ways that I reflected and wrote about my thinking, experiences and inquiries. As a child in Romania I documented recordings of my learning using mainly narratives, and as a teacher in Israel I documented my students' learning via data collections and analyses. As a research scientist in the laboratory, I reviewed professional literature in the area of research and designed new experiments to answer essential research questions. Because in scientific research one may not be able to compare and contrast results with available literature, multiple repetitions of the same experiment provide the comparative elements. As a research scientist one learns that repetitions, although intended to be identical repetitions, may yield different results. Coming to the USA for a PhD in Science Education drew my attention away from expressing learning via narrative (as I did in Romania) and narrative-"free" short science research articles written in the third person in which science was reported as a linear process starting with the research question, followed by the materials and methods, the findings, results, and conclusions (also called "scientific method" in science teaching) (as I did in Israel) to a new way of expressing learning in science education using metacognition and pattern formations.

The theoretical worldview in this chapter represents this new framework, one that uses professional literature to question and scaffold learning in a field such as, in this book, the dynamics of my worldview on schooling and on learning and teaching science and mathematics. After the next section on my life as a child in Romania, I present my theoretical perspective on worldview, which is then followed by my worldview on schooling in the USA.

My roots are in socialist Romania, my worldview on schooling, and the learning and teaching of science and mathematics began there. Romania in the 1960s was what I considered the norm for many years. For this reason in this chapter I have decided to present a narrative representing a day in my life as a child in Romania.

A DAY FROM MY LIFE AS A CHILD IN SOCIALIST ROMANIA IN THE 1960S

Hedy! Wake up! Time to go to school! My grandma would yell every morning, and on the tenth time she is waiting for me to get out of bed. Well, after having to solve more problems from the Olivotto collection to satisfy after staying awake until 2 am this morning to solve more problems from the Olivotto collection to satisfy Ms. Bayer's requirements, it is no surprise that I can hardly open my eyes at 7. Of course, neither did playing on the street until 11 pm last night. I really don't understand why we have to solve problems created for students in grades 4-7 while we are students in grade 3. I know that with Ms. Bayer my complaint will not work anyway, especially if she talks with my father.

Well, I should get ready more quickly as I want to meet all my friends, and it is getting late. I try to avoid cleaning teeth, however my grandma is watching me like a hawk and has the toothbrush and paste ready as she watches me brush... I dress up and on my way to school talk with my friends and plan the play for school breaks and afternoon games.

I have only one mistake in my reading and a dictation quiz since I forget to write the second "c" in cinci – meaning five – why can't we just use the figure five? Ms. Bayer requires us again to write every letter in a calligraphic way AND SPELL CORRECTLY while she is dictating as she is speaking – no slowing down!!! What else? Well, for the arithmetic problems from Olivotto she wants us to show every step in our thinking and have it correctly solved. She is really tough, but then I should be used to her after three years.

Planting a few seeds according to our choice from the ones that germinated in the last project, beginning to water them and collecting data on their growth was not too bad – I bet that the ones planted in the shady areas will be smaller, look worse, or even die. Let's see.

Sports for the last period—what a treat!!! We change into PE (physical education) clothes—I think Ionel is peeking to see the girls undress, but then, if I say that I see Ionel peeking, it might be interpreted I am watching to see him peeking (Figure 1.1).

Figure 1.1. Boy peeking into girl's locker room.

We have only one room where we can change our clothes for PE, and the boys in our class do a pretty good job keeping the boys from the other classes from peeking at us. I play basketball again during PE – a real treat as during breaks the third graders don't stand a chance against kids in seventh and eighth grades, even if they know how to play.

A little before noon, I am on my way home with friends. It is good that today is a short day as tomorrow we study until 1 pm, followed by piano lesson and a good lunch prepared by grandma, a little homework, and then German language with Ms. Deutsch, then PLAY. Maybe I can play sick and not go to Ms. Deutsch? But then, I will not be allowed to play. Well, one has to do what one has to do. Good that Daniela does my drawings for tomorrow in exchange for my doing mathematics homework for today – less time spent on useless trials, and my mom is not too good at drawing either! It is crazy that my parents cannot help me with the stupid drawings – funny, when my mom did it she received an even lower grade that I did. Thanks, Daniela! Finally, time to play — got my ball and tennis shoes—I am ready for a fun afternoon and evening.

Five friends call my name from under my window. Grandma announces that I am still doing homework. Free time, finally! I go to play lots of games with children and teenagers living close-by. We make group selections according to one's record with these games. I am pretty good with all ballgames so I serve as team captain for many games and taking turns, select my team of players. As night hours approach, I wish that father would have more work to do and stay later, but he is the one asking me to go in the house, take a shower, eat something and go to sleep. At 10:30 pm he appears and calls me – lucky that my friends ask for "another five minutes to finish the game." At 11 pm father calls again and I have to go in, attempting to sneak to my room, as I am too tired to shower and eat. However, he is determined to make me shower. Well, after a short shower I go to bed.

MY LIFE IN SOCIALIST ROMANIA

Being born and growing up in socialist Romania until age 17 was mainly a matter of biology/genetics during the time that Nicolae Ceausescu succeeded Gheorghe Gheorghiu-Dej in leading Romania towards socialism after 1965. While I did not have anything to do with the biology involved in my creation and birth, Ceausescu was the one who refused permission that would have allowed our family to emigrate from Romania and go to Israel where most of our extended family was living.

My childhood and teen years in Romania were occupied with two main things: play and education. Play involved meeting with neighborhood children and teenagers in front of my block of flats and playing until most of us could not avoid our parents' callings and ultimatums. Education involved meeting the neighborhood youth in school, preparing, applying and succeeding in being accepted to the high school of our choice, going to movies, plays, and concerts, attending Olympiads (i.e., high school competitions in different areas of expertise such as mathematics, chemistry, etc.), and reading and discussing books.

Growing up in socialist Romania had advantages and disadvantages. The advantages were mainly in the area of education, since studies for grades 1-12, as well as books for all the subjects were free of charge. Entrance examinations before ninth grade that included written and oral testing in Romanian, Mathematics, and Romanian History (only oral) determined the high school level one was able to attend - from highly academic to technical school. After graduating from high school, once admitted to the university, a student could study for free but would have to purchase textbooks (that were very cheap and affordable). In exchange, once students finished their studies they were sent to fill available jobs, usually in small cities and villages for a number of years. Movies, opera, books, concerts, theater performances, all were very affordable and heavily subsidized by the state.

Another advantage was the emphasis on developing all skills for all students. Our schooling from first to eighth grade took place in the same school building, and we all studied Romanian, foreign languages, social sciences, science, mathematics, physical education, home economics (e.g., cooking, sewing, working with woods and metals), music, and the arts – there was no differentiation according to gender or socioeconomic status in terms of expectations. There was praise for excellent results in any of these areas. As students stayed in the same class during grades 1-8, we learned to rely on each other and work together, while at the same time compete for first, second and third prizes, given each year to the best students in the class based on grade point average that included academics (oral and written performances) and behavior. As all neighborhood children attended the same school, we all had access to the same teachers. Because of the law that gypsies had to send their children to school up to the tenth grade, gender and race did not matter in terms of academic or sports opportunities and achievements.

Vertical stratification of the floors in the blocks of flats allowed families with different incomes to live in the same building. Families with the lowest income inhabited the floor that was mostly underground with a small window allowing for sunlight to lighten the rooms. First and second floors were the most expensive and the apartment price/rent went down for the third and fourth floors. Population density was also a factor such that lower socioeconomic families inhabited higher density small buildings where there would be three to four individuals per room. However, for children playing in the street, socioeconomics did not matter; instead what mattered were the other children's ability and availability to play games.

On the list of disadvantages of growing up in Romania, first place goes to the lack of freedom (e.g., not being allowed to emigrate to Israel, or even go on a trip outside Romania with the whole family) and having to pretend that socialism and communism were the best ways to live, despite our knowledge of capitalistic societies via tourists and family or friends who emigrated to other countries. There was also the fear of being discovered by the "securitate" and being locked in prisons or sentenced to death. The statement, "Even the walls have ears" was used to limit the conversations to accepted topics, just in case security spies were among us.

Questions Set 1.1:

1. Reflect and write two to three paragraphs showing similarities and differences between my educational/schooling system and the one in which you grew up. Focus on diversity in student population and expectations in terms of learning for all students.
2. Reflect and write two to three paragraphs, using vertical versus horizontal stratification and its implications[1], on the sociocultural aspects of your growing up. Who were the kids with whom you played/socialized, when did you play, and what were the relationships with other kids' parents?
3. Discuss your answers to the questions in small groups and then share with class. Organize the class information using a table and/or text. Summarize main ideas and show connections between the table and written paragraphs.

WORLDVIEW THEORY

It is difficult to decide how far to go back in history for the time and location that worldview theory began. Should we begin with Lao-Tse who is considered the father of the Taoist school (WebChron, 2010) and defined Te (meaning virtue), a sense of morality, as the main ingredient for a person's function? The Taoist school looks at expressing morality without expecting retribution, i.e., the rewards and penances in a future life. Or should we go further back into Judaism and find the worldviews described in these ancient writings?

I have decided to begin with the instances in which worldview was mentioned in a review article summarizing the work done on this subject up to 1975. In a literature review, Kearney (1975) defines different phases in worldview research using different lenses. According to Kearney, a *formative* phase (using a cultural historical lens) is followed by a *transitional* phase (using an anthropological lens), and later by a *propositional* phase (using more of an analytical lens). Kearney explains his approach as combining the different lenses and using a *systematic* approach "in which there is greater concern to explore the kinds of dynamic relationships that integrate the various isolated propositions of particular worldviews among themselves, their social and geographic environments, and their associated cultural behaviours" (p. 267). Almost a decade later, Kearney revisits his previous worldview definition and emphasizes the need for multiple lenses to define such a complex concept. He defines worldview as a "culturally organized macrothought: those dynamically inter-related basic assumptions of a people that determine much of their behavior and decision-making, as well as organizing much of their body of symbolic creations ... and ethnophilosophy in general" (1984, p. 1).

Aerts et al. (2007) concur with Kearney's view and define worldview as "a coherent collection of concepts and theorems that must allow us to construct a global image of the world, and in this way to understand as many elements of our experience as possible" (p. 8). In other words, how we perceive the world is filtered through our personal sifting system that contains personal elements and criteria. Vidal (2008) finds worldview and philosophy in its broadest sense as "closely related," when he says "worldview crowns philosophy" (p. 3). Wikipedia (2010) uses a large number of references and addresses worldview as having its roots in the German Weltanschauung (Welt = world, and Anschauung = view or outlook). Worldview is defined as the "fundamental cognitive orientation of an individual or society" using various lenses such as natural philosophy, fundamental existential norms, values, emotions, and ethics.

In the area of science education, Cobern (1991) describes worldview as fundamental assumptions that direct and provide meaning for actions in the different subcultures in which the individual is active. In a given situation, actions might have different interpretations according to the worldviews of the participants that filter observations. To illustrate this idea, Cobern uses the example in which student and teacher's worldviews about a concept in science differ. The teacher uses various techniques in her efforts (unsuccessfully, on many occasions) to accommodate student's worldview to fit with her own. Later, Cobern (1994) emphasizes the "nonrational" or subconscious aspect of these fundamental assumptions that ultimately ground the individual's conceptions of reality. Cobern states, "A worldview is the set of fundamental non-rational presuppositions on which these conceptions of reality are grounded" (p. 6). It is possible for an individual to follow and understand a rational process, but this understanding does not necessarily translate into a change in a person's worldview. First published in 1936, Einstein (2003) portrays science as a changing entity and the scientist as a "poor philosopher" (p. 22) who is producing "some sort of order among sense impressions, this order being produced by the creation of general concepts, relations between these concepts, and by definite relations of some kind between these concepts and sense experience" (p. 24). Einstein's view on science (and physics, in particular) is confirmed by Glasersfeld's perspective on the nature of science as dynamic and human-dependent (1988, 1991a).

In the area of mathematics education, Schoenfeld (2003) explores how a teacher's worldviews are reflected via practices in the classrooms. In his article entitled *The math wars,* Schoenfeld (2004) provides an excellent example with a situation in which "traditionalists" and "reform-oriented" mathematicians do not hold the same worldviews regarding mathematics education, each group promoting its own position as the "right' one. In other words, even if individuals find their subject (in this case mathematics) equally important, they might hold different worldviews as to the most effective ways to educate students in this area. Also in the area of mathematics education I need to mention Glasersfeld's edited book entitled *Radical Constructivism in Mathematics Education* (1991b), in which mathematics educators describe classroom research at different schooling levels on teaching mathematics from elementary school to college level and in different areas of mathematics. Schoenfeld summarizes basic book principles in the introductory chapter, supporting the assumption that "knowledge is the result of learner's activity" (p. xiv) and the underlying importance of students' experiences in the process of learning. While he does not deny an objective "reality," Glasersfeld questions our ability to access and describe it, as we all have our personal lenses based on personal experiences.

MY WORLDVIEW ON SCHOOLING IN ROMANIA

As I was born and raised in Romania, my worldview was strongly influenced by established norms present at that time in Romania. For example, I understood "schooling" as a social event in which gender and socioeconomic status did not count. The school day was divided into educational and recreational time with educational time requiring intellectual involvement (sometimes taken to the extreme with solving the Olivotto arithmetic challenges), and recreation time ruled by physical abilities. Collaboration and collegiality were encouraged, even when we competed for the first, second and third prizes at the classroom levels, or later in high school for the Olympiad prizes. Group learning, peer tutoring, and collaboration on projects came naturally in this environment, and we learned to work together for an established common goal. Success in mathematics and science was also independent of gender and socioeconomic status. What usually counted was the ability to think, and time spent on these subjects. Teachers were always willing to answer any student's questions, and they treated students' questions with respect. Both students and parents treated teachers respectfully, and teachers usually lived in the same community in which they taught. Being neighbors, teachers had the advantage of knowing students' parents and the disadvantage of having to talk about their students when meeting the parents at the local stores.

While students in Romania took educational advantages for granted (e.g., cheap tickets to educational and cultural events, free education and free books during first to twelfth grade schooling), we were not blind to the advantages of capitalism and the effects of the "securitate" police on our lives. The lack of freedom to speak openly and restrictions on travelling outside Romania bothered high school students in the early 1970s, especially when we had to say something that we did not believe, for the purpose of getting good grades in subjects such as Contemporary History and Political Sciences.

Questions Set 1.2:

1. Using narrative, describe in writing your initial sociocultural worldview, based on your experiences in the society in which you grew up (in two to three paragraphs).
2. Compare your worldview with those of your group members. Do you see common points? Differences? Develop a table summarizing these elements.

3.   As a class, collect and look (via an organized table) at the worldviews of the different participants.

It is interesting to point out that one is able to differentiate between the elements of the worldview only because of the dissonance created by later experiences or by listening to peers' descriptions of their worldviews. If we are born, grow, and live our lives all in the same community, we become blind to the norms, even if these norms change over time. Reflection is necessary in order to identify differences in the worldview created by slow modifications over time.

DYNAMICS OF MY WORLDVIEW REGARDING SCHOOLING

Israel

I spent 18 years in Israel, with more than 17 of these years in Jerusalem. If I were to record the most memorable experiences related to the country and schooling, I would choose my experience in the city of Petah Tikva during the Yom Kippur war in 1973 (a few months after my arrival to Israel) and the semester conferences with the other teachers talking about student achievements.

Yom Kippur War

For my first Yom Kippur in Israel, I fast with my uncle and his family and go to the local Ashkenazi synagogue for the Erev Yom Kippur service (Jewish holydays actually begin at sundown the day before and last until the first visible star or at dark). "You see, no one is driving on Yom Kippur," my uncle says. "We all stay at home with the family. No one is working tomorrow and no one is driving anywhere until Yom Kippur ends after dark." "Wow! What an experience," I am thinking. And while we are walking toward the synagogue it is true. No cars, all the children play in the streets, adults walk. No cars. After the service, however, I begin seeing cars. "Ha!" I say. "You told me there are no cars and I can see some." So, Israelis are not really keeping Yom Kippur   it is like in Romania where people have fewer cars, therefore less traffic." "Something is wrong," said my uncle. When we arrive home, an urgent military order for him to show up for service is waiting. Later that night we hear the first siren announcing to go into the "miklat" or shelter underneath the house. My uncle's family, including the children, is ready in less than ten minutes. They are ready to leave the house while I am still brushing my teeth and taking my time to think about items I need to take with me. "There is no time for that," my grandma tells me, and my younger cousin takes me patiently by the hand and we go downstairs to the shelter.

The following days prove to be very challenging, as following the sirens, we spend a lot of time in the shelter. We are not allowed to use lights for fear of getting bombed, as a lighted city could be identified easily from the sky by enemy airplanes. We have the windows covered in one room, which allows us watch the news on TV, and the family is there to eat and to support one another. It is frightening, as we do not hear anything about my uncle. During the nights, I join my aunt who is the director of the microbiology laboratory at a local firm and volunteers at the local hospital. Individuals driving slowly during the night, who without lights, would stop and ask us where we need to go, and everybody functions as a large and caring family. There is a sense of togetherness that goes beyond words and individuals go out of their way to help each other.

Teacher Conferences at the School Site

In Israel I studied at the Hebrew University in Jerusalem and finished a BSc in Science/Biology, and MSc in Microbiology (Parasitology), with life credentials to teach science, biology, and mathematics in grades 7-12. My experience with teacher conferences opens my eyes to the teaching culture in Israel and the importance of every student.

At the time for midterms and before student conferences with parents (Figure 1.2), all the teachers who teach a certain class or part of the class have to show up for a meeting. We sit around an oval table; there are more than 15 teachers, a counselor, and the nurse who are attending every meeting. The reason for having so many teachers teaching each student is that subjects are taught for different number of periods/six-days week, from one time to many times per week. For example, Physical Education is usually twice per week for one hour each time, while Mathematics counts for five hours per week, two for Geometry, and three for Algebra or other combinations. The secretary already had entered midterm grades anonymously, and during the meeting we discuss every student in depth. Needless to say, we find that some students who do very poorly in some subjects excel in others. We learn about difficult home situations and, as a group discuss ways to improve the student's chances to succeed. Respect for every student is essential, and understanding them helps us to assist many students to stay out of trouble. Since part of the principal's job is teaching, our principal is present at many of the meetings as a teacher of record and discusses the specific student with us. Every teacher has a voice that is heard, and these discussions help me understand that every student/child needs not only a village but also a committed group of teachers to educate them and help them achieve their potential to go one step further (stretch). It is always an issue of pushing children to achieve more than they think they can. I also understand the meaning of the saying, "Teach every child as if she were your own."

While I am teaching and talking about improvement for every student in my classroom, other groups are discussing similar services for my own boys. Looping (i.e., the same teacher teaching a group of students for multiple sequential years) and using teachers already in the school to substitute for absent teachers ensures quality and consistency in meeting educational goals for our students.

Figure 1.2. Teachers conversing about their students.

Expansion of my worldview of schooling

New country, new language, new culture! While it is expected to have to learn to express ideas in a new language, Hebrew is very different from Romanian. Different characters, words are written from right to left, and vowels are partially absent in the accepted written communication (appearing only in biblical writings and in materials written for the new immigrants). In Israel, vertical as well as horizontal stratification systems work simultaneously, determining house prices and rents, and accordingly, socioeconomic profiles. While elementary and middle school site selection depends on the school boundaries similar to the U.S. educational system, high school studies are more competitive and students are allowed to apply to very highly regarded high schools according to each student's grade point average (GPA). Gender does not affect students' success in schools, and both males and females are expected to succeed in their state-mandated matriculation examinations based on areas of interest, and to enroll in Israeli's army service by the end of high school for two to three years (two years for girls, and three for boys). During the mandatory army service individuals do not receive a salary, just a minimal allowance mainly for travel expenses when soldiers visit home. Following army service, Israeli citizens can be called to serve in the army for up to 60 days per year and they receive their salary during this period. In order to begin studies at the university and prepare for the entrance examinations, individuals enroll in a preparatory course or study on their own. Entry examinations for superior studies at the university are usually in the form of a psychotechnic examination based on pattern recognition. Some majors (e.g.,

Biology) require an additional examination of basic knowledge in the area and ability to use information provided in various forms for problem-solving.

First to twelfth grade education in Israel is mandatory. Since families do not pay for the education, they must purchase schoolbooks (relatively inexpensive, especially for the used ones) and additional tools required by the teacher (e.g., protractor, pencils, and notebooks). Socioeconomic differentiation has an effect on students' clothing, quality of their materials, Internet access, and reliance on help with school issues at home (e.g., private tutor). In Israel, a country of immigrants, there seems to be a differentiation between the Ashkenazi and Sephardi subgroups (based on historical origin) in the socioeconomic sense and on their views on education, although with mixed subgroup marriages the differences begin to blur. In Israel, there is also a relatively clear correlation between education and socioeconomic status.

To summarize, in Israel the expansion of my worldview on schooling included realizing that elementary school can be restricted to first to fifth grade, followed by middle school for grades sixth to eighth, and high school for ninth to twelfth grade. In this system, students get regrouped for their middle school years and for their high school experience. Most neighborhoods show a variety of socioeconomic levels due to vertical and horizontal stratifications. Socioeconomics may play a role in the student population in neighborhood elementary and middle schools, with more assistance and higher education possible for the families who can hire tutors to help their children. While the curriculum is set for the whole country, specific teachers or teachers' groups in a school choose books and other required materials. GPAs and teacher recommendations count for high school acceptance, sometimes accompanied by testing results.

Although not directly related to schooling, safety of the country and being surrounded by enemy countries connect all the citizens of Israel together. Having high expectations for every child is at the foundation of the educational system, and every child is educated to become a leader.

United States of America

I arrived in the USA in 1991 to pursue a Ph.D. in Science Education at Florida State University, under the leadership of Professor Ken Tobin, a well-known science educator, whom Israeli science educators had recommended to me. While I was involved in my studies, my husband, Uri, and I were involved in our sons' schooling (ages four, eight, and twelve). School boundaries determined the student population for K-12 education system in Tallahassee, Florida, USA. The University Student Housing (where we resided) was located in a low socioeconomic area. My second son, Tal, enrolled to attend the local elementary school, while my oldest son, Danny attended the local middle school. My youngest son, Ido, attended the preschool situated inside the university-run, housing complex.

The parents in the university housing complex would inform new arrivals about the best teachers in the local public schools and procedures required to apply for changes, groups to join (e.g., City Council, Parent-Teacher Organization for schools), and major programs affecting our children's education (e.g., English

Language Learning programs in Florida, Mathematics Enrichment). International parents were more than willing to share what they knew and our collegiality went beyond advice into strong friendships and almost co-parenting.

Horizontal stratification and school boundaries determined the schools that one's offspring would attend. As we were living in a majority African-American, low socioeconomic area, our sons attended schools with low expectations from the local population. School education was for the "working class" to use Anyon's framework (1980, 1997) and was taught by "working class" teachers. Following and enforcing established rules, monitoring the completion of worksheets requiring no intellectual involvement, and discouraging student voice characterized the schools' atmosphere. There was gender differentiation with girls being discouraged from performing "brainy" tasks (e.g., in science and mathematics) or sports (e.g., playing basketball). (see Figure 1.3) As expected from children of graduate students raised in an atmosphere in which the children had a voice (sometimes even more than one per child!) and aspirations, problems began to arise and we international parents were constantly called to schools to solve the "misbehavior" of our children. We demanded a different kind of education than the education for the "working class" to fit our goals for our children. On one occasion we (mainly international parents) threatened the superintendent's office with a parent strike attended by local journalists in order to replace an inefficient principal at the local middle school. The principal was moved to another school for one year followed by his retirement.

To summarize, in our schooling experience in Tallahassee, Florida, in light of the larger culture and due to horizontal stratification, we saw differentiation based on socioeconomics and even gender. Low socioeconomic strata have access to "working class" education (Anyon, 1980, 1997), and girls are expected to take care of their outside appearance rather than their brain and athletic abilities.

Figure 1.3. Hedy as a young woman in Romania in the 1960s and young woman now in USA with her cell phone.

In Florida, school buses pick up students and take them to school (for safety and equity reasons) and subsidize the students' breakfast and lunch, according to parents' income. Only on Fridays do classes for all subjects meet for periods of 50 minutes; on Mondays and Wednesdays, half of the classes for subjects meet for extended periods, and on Tuesday and Thursdays the other half of the classes for subjects meet for extended periods. Schools provide books for the different subjects free of charge for the pre-kindergarten to twelfth grade students on a "rental" agreement. Principals generally do not teach, resulting in most cases in a separation between teaching and administrative groups. After school sports and competitions among schools begin in middle schools and continue during high school years. Universities continue the sport tradition by recruiting and supporting the education of the best athletic candidates. Safety issues are local, usually restricted to gang actions or alcohol or drug abuse. Army service is not mandatory, and individuals receive pay for service in the military.

In Romania and Israel, with the exception of some self-contained classrooms, students stayed in their classroom and the teachers migrated to the students. In the USA we found the opposite situation, with students rushing during the five-minute break between classes to exchange books from lockers, and reach classrooms for the next period in a different room.

Questions Set 1.3:

1. Identify educational and societal goals underlying the different school systems described in this chapter.
2. Reflect and write two to three paragraphs describing the dynamics of your worldview with respect to the concept of schooling (i.e., initial, class worldview, text narratives).
3. If you could build an ideal schooling system, what would it look like? Use Think, Ink, Pair, Share (Reflect, write ideas down, share with group members around the same table, share main ideas with class).

WORLDVIEW ON LEARNING AND TEACHING SCIENCE AND MATHEMATICS

My worldview regarding science and mathematics learning and teaching is based on my experiences in the different countries in which I lived and visited. I see worldview as dynamic—specific to time and space while allowing fluent movement among mini cultures in which we hold membership (Kearney, 1975) and over time with mixing/changing cultures (Aerts et al., 2007; Cobern, 1993; Kearney, 1975). With each additional experience, our worldview requires adaptation either reinforcing known patterns (Jean Piaget's assimilation) or challenging known patterns through disequilibrium and required readdressing and modifying/expanding our personal worldview (Piaget's accommodation) (Cherry, 2010).

Worldview does not evolve in a vacuum. As social beings, we need to acknowledge the human element mediating the processes of making sense of experiences. As we interact with others, we clarify our own positions and expand our understanding – we learn and change. Reading the works of Vygotsky (1978) on the social aspects of learning, Bauersfeld (1988) on the interactions among individuals in mathematics education, and Tobin (1993a) in science education provided me with the tools and elements necessary to uncover my worldview regarding science and mathematics learning and teaching.

THIS BOOK AND THE TWENTYFIRST CENTURY SKILLS

This book documents my exploration of my worldview of science and mathematics learning and teaching, based upon my experiences of living in three continents, and in light of the requirements of the citizenry living in the global community of the 21st century. I was first introduced to *The Partnership for the 21st Century Skills* group's work a few years ago at a mini-conference on assessments in the areas of science. One of the group's members advocated for new questions to be asked and answered in order to prepare high school graduates (in the USA, I found their picture of the high school graduate to be universal for the global community) for the 21st century skills— skills considerably different from those of the 20th century (The Partnership for the 21st Century Skills, 2006). With new global challenges and changes such as the nature of education, competition, and the nature of jobs, all skills have to change. In order for a high school graduate to be competitive, the group recommends six areas of change: 1) core subjects, 2) 21st century content, learning and thinking skills, 3) Information and Communication Technology (ICT), 4) literacy, 5) life skills, and 6) 21st century assessments. The subcategories of the areas of change look at developing intellectual abilities as well as developing social skills, and being able to live a healthy life. I was especially drawn to the "life skills" area, which encompassed leadership, ethics, accountability, adaptability, personal productivity, personal responsibility, people skills, self-direction and social responsibility (p. 1), as necessary subcategories. These abilities and skills, according to me, really define a human being. In a recently published document (The Partnership for the 21st Century Skills, 2009), the authors begin with questions about our students: "Are your students critical thinkers? Problem-solvers? Good communicators? Good collaborators? Information and technology literate? Flexible and adaptable? Innovative and creative? Globally competent? Environmentally literate?" Needless to say, it will take the whole global community commitment to educate our children and us to become global citizens of the 21st century.

On the same subject, stemming from investigation of the new technology savvy student population, reserachers propose a new definition of socializing (sociotechnology), even job requirements, and changes required from schools and systems to accommodate the new demands in a book edited by Jacobs (2010), the master of interdisciplinary curriculum. From the ICT area, Kozma (2005) defines the global ICT-based education reform as requiring policy changes to support the new directions. Using alternative policies applied in Singapore (focusing on economic growth) and Finland (focusing on social development), the author uncovers the process that brought these countries success in education and proposes a framework for ICT-based educational, economic, and social development. Kozma's recommendations in curricular reform, pedagogical reform, and assessment reform have implications for teacher professional development, school organization, and systemic reform and educational transformation. On the subject of curriculum reform, Kozma supports using a knowledge creation approach with associated skills and habits "that include information management communication, working in teams, entrepreneurialism, global awareness, civic engagement, problem-solving, using technology, and design systems" (p. 38). For pedagogical reform, Kozma shifts the teaching from the dispensing of knowledge to using inquiry and problem-solving approaches and demanding from the students that they identify problems, design solutions, and communicate the results in communities of learners.

Moore, Fowler, Jesiek, Moore and Watson (2008) discuss requirements in fluency in instructional technology (FITness) and learner-centered practices for learners in higher education. They emphasize maximizing using learner-centered practice when implementing change/innovations (i.e., the concern-based adoption model) to guide new learning processes. For 21st century learning, we need to 1) teach students to be productive in immersive, interdisciplinary learning groups, and 2) build infrastructure to support FITness development.

The National Science Teachers Association (NSTA, 2011) agrees, as found in its position statement that 21st century skills include: "learning and innovation skills; information, media, and technology skills; life and career skills; adaptability; complex communication/social skills; nonroutine problem solving; self-management/self-development; and systems thinking" (p. 1).

My worldview on learning and teaching science and mathematics evolved during many years. In the following chapters I emphasize the ingredients that I find necessary for education in these areas. My view takes into consideration the student population with whom I have worked, and my learning through attending conferences in a variety of countries around the globe.

NOTES

[1] For information on vertical versus horizontal stratification, see this link: http://www.sociologyguide.com/social-mobility/types-of-mobility.php.

WHAT DO YOU MEAN, YOU KNOW SCIENCE AND MATHEMATICS?

INTRODUCTION

This chapter explores the meaning and processes of learning science and mathematics, and the meaning of being fluent in these subjects in a global society. Since the processes of learning, understanding and knowing are internal to individuals, societies have created external expressions of understandings to provide some kind of measurement to compare individuals' knowledge expressions in classrooms and among classrooms in the same school, different schools, regional areas in the same country, as well as in countries. With the evolving global community and the need to prepare citizenry for the 21st century, these external expressions of peoples' learning, understanding and knowing science and mathematics have extended beyond societies into the global arena.

Because we attempt to quantify people's learning, understanding and knowledge in science and mathematics at the pre-college levels as the means for comparison and improvement, this chapter also analyzes a variety of the external expressions called tests, assessments and/or evaluations in different societies and their evolution with time.

BEFORE SCHOOL ERA – FOCUS ON EARLY CHILDHOOD EDUCATION

There is no question regarding the importance of the first years in every child's life. As infants struggle through various aspects of communication and mastering motor skills, their brains evolve and learn. Constructive interactions with the environment are essential during this development and, as Enfield (2010) points out, infants' thinking is visible via "communication without syntax," meaning that communication happens via the use of body language and facial expressions. Needless to say, the picture (Enfield, 2010, p. 1600) showing interaction among three infants is an example of communication that is both initiated and responded to without using words. Enfield (2010) argues against biolinguists, such as Chomsky and Fitch, stating that language evolution begins with "communication without syntax" (p. 1601) during infancy.

Of course, I am not going to solve the above-mentioned linguistic evolutionary dilemma or discuss the biochemical pathway of the behavioral and emotional expressions of infants in this book. The fact is that with verbal development, infants begin to use words and sentences that they hear during their nonverbal period, hinting toward the development of cognitive constructs.

As an example, one of my sons would say the word "todah" meaning "thank you" in Hebrew, extending the hand to receive an item he wanted. Interestingly enough, he was using his body language and facial expression to supply the additional information for the item he wanted to receive. While conceptually he knew exactly what he wanted and why (trying to provide him with a different item resulting in crying and noisy expressions of frustration), the words and the "syntax" associated with the verbal asking were missing.

Every day we hear about miracle learners. Mothers and researchers use expressions such as "Young children are like sponges when it comes to learning," or "You cannot believe it – my daughter reads and she is only 4 years old!" What happens here? Do some children have a certain gene or tendency to learn while others do not possess this? From my personal experience I know that all children learn, however, they might choose something that is different from the adult's intended learning, which actually does not get checked or quantified. The learning experience needs to be relevant to the child, relevant enough to convince her to invest time and energy – to get involved.

Learning About Flux, Reflux, and the Changing Sea

I was very young when, during the summer months, I joined my father on his trips to the Black Sea shore where he was performing as a pianist or an accordion player, to supplement his diminished income as an engineer. The cut in salary was Ceausescu's way to punish individuals who attempted to emigrate from Romania to be with their families. My father, who held the same position as the head of a building project, would sit in the same chair and perform the same duties. However his salary was cut to one-third the head's salary.

As my father enjoyed taking a short morning nap on the sunny beach after a night of performing with the band, I was left to beach explorations. Of course, I had been given my instructions not to go into the water alone, to stay within a very short distance from our beach spot, and play with the sand and toys he was diligently bringing, etc.... I felt free once he fell asleep. My preferred adventure spots were the fishing pier and the sea. The reason for calling these adventures spots is understandable when one takes into consideration the many mishaps that happened during these times. Fishermen began to know me as I was continuously asking questions related to fishing and often falling from the slippery rocks into the waters. As I was not a great swimmer despite my father's efforts to teach me, dealing with waves and rocks near the fishing pier was beyond my abilities. Fishermen kept an eye on me and would jump into the water to save me on a regular basis.

The tricky sea would also take me into deeper waters when I was entering the water to "just fill the bucket with water." On numerous occasions, at a very young age, I recall water closing above my head. As I would look upward to the sun and try to keep my breath, I would see that the seawater was of a lighter color, a light blue. I also knew that I needed to move and get back to land while trying to attract adults' attention. On many occasions I made it to safety on my own and felt very happy that I did not have to convince an adult not to tell my father about the little escapade. The swimming lessons with instructors as well as with my father paid off in the long run as they kept me alive. Other times, adults would insist on bringing me to my father and I often got punished for not listening to him. The result? I finally learned that the sea was tricky and changing, and never to go in the deep part without another person present.

Learning About Proportions

Here is a situation in which I had to use arithmetic, namely proportions, in order to make sure that my cousin, one year older than me, would not cheat me with candies bought with both of our moneys. I was not in school yet, however proportions seemed easy when it came to counting candies and getting the correct share. I recall "one for me, two for you" when he spent double the money I had. I even recall the different candies we bought, from chocolate covered peanuts to sugar candies, when we had to take into consideration how large the pieces were in addition to the absolute number. In this situation, I encountered the concept of remainder that could not be divided according to proportion and still keep the candies intact.

This story shows us that experiences during the early years of our lives remain with us forever. Skills that we learned to use during these years improve with time (such as mental math), and fears that we developed also remain (such as fear of being alone in deep waters).

Questions Set 2.1:

1. Do you recall a similar informal experience(s) before you started school, when you learned science and/or mathematics, using relevant and engaging experiences? Needless to say, the experience(s) do not have to be as dramatic and life threatening as my experience with sea-related phenomena. Write one to two paragraphs.
2. Discuss in small groups similarities and differences between the experiences shared and write one to two paragraphs summarizing them.
3. Create a table of experiences as a class and connect the experiences to the learning of science and mathematics concepts. Describe feelings associated with the experience/skill.

CONCRETE TO ABSTRACT MOVEMENT AND THE MEANING OF HIGH EXPECTATIONS IN SCHOOLING

As a science teacher and educator, I have had to shift from simply using abstract knowledge to also using concrete knowledge (Figure 2.1) when teaching my students, whether I was a K-12 teacher or a teacher educator of prospective and practicing teachers. My prior experiences in teaching and learning shaped my worldview, enabling me to help students to transition from concrete to abstract knowledge.

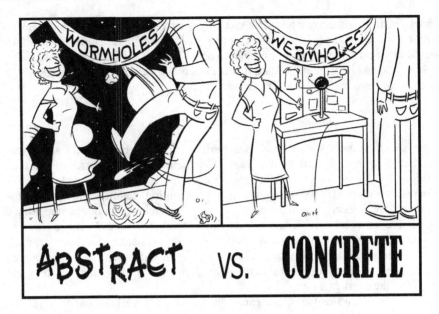

Figure 2.1. Hedy... grappling with teaching and learning.

Mrs. Bayer Charmed Us to Think

Looking back at my early school years in grades one to three, I was lucky to have had Ms. Bayer as a teahcer. She worked with the whole child, her parents, with the class and school community to push "her children's" education forward. In her eyes, all children could learn and exceed the expectations of the relatively mediocre general schooling requirements (according to her). Early on she identified the slackers in the classrom and she knew methods to convince them to move forward without forcing them – just by giving them a challenge.

Here is an example of how Ms. Bayer would use her charm to make us think in first grade.

> Arithmetic time – I love it. Somehow mental mathematics and common sense help me with the problems in the book as well as with the exercises. I have some issues with having to show her my work, as it is boring once I know the final result that is usually correct.

> Ms. Bayer comes in with an uncut loaf of white regular bread, places it on her desk, measures it, and then cuts it into two halves. She asks us to tell her how much of the loaf is each part – very easy, it is half. Buying bread at the local bread store had already taught me and my friends the meaning of half a loaf of bread, as the seller often had to cut the long white bread or the round dark bread into halves for different customers (usually the elderly neighbors who lived alone). "Good," she says. "Now I have a challenge. I need to divide this

loaf in three equal parts and give one piece to each one of my neighbors. Any ideas as to what I should do?" At this point, Ms. Bayer asks each one of us to think and find a solution and write it down. I recall the challenge. As I do not want to mess up the bread by trying different things, I draw the bread as a line in my notebook and make the half cut. I draw another line underneath this one and cut it into three equal pieces. The drawings do not fit in terms of cuts. After a few more minutes, Ms. Bayer asks us to close the arithmetic notebook and take out another subject. Unfortunately, I could not close my mind in the same way and continue to try and solve the mathematics puzzle while pretending to listen to Ms. Bayer. All day long I think about cutting the bread until I figure out a solution cutting the bread halves into three pieces each, and giving two pieces to each of the three neighbors. In first grade I do not know about writing fractions, so I do not translate the $1/6 + 1/6 = 2/6$ or, if simplified, $1/3$. What I do understand, however, is that cutting it into six equal pieces would allow me to use the half cut and still be able to cut the loaf into three equal pieces.

Ms. Bayer had students come to the board, divide the loaf on the board into numerous parts, and show the way in which we solved the problem with all the necessary steps. Comparing and contrasting different ways of thinking as well as drawing the problem also showed us that different ways of thinking were just different, not better or worse. Later in my life I realized that Ms. Bayer was using a teaching technique called "Think, Ink, Pair, Share" to challenge us to think and record our thinking before sharing our ideas with others.

Ms. Bayer's high expectations proved to be a continuously challenging mechanism that kept us using our brains while transitioning from the already cut bread halves (concrete) experiences into dividing the bread into three equal pieces without actually cutting it (abstract). Ms. Bayer's greatness lay in her ability to teach abstract concepts while providing the necessary concrete examples to get students to use previous experiences stored in our memories, especially when we were in the first grade. For example, she illustrated the connection between 10 groups of one and one group of ten by removing and placing an elastic band around ten burned matches, which we were using as manipulatives in first grade. Slowly we (students) began developing our own creations in order to illustrate concepts, such as drawing a line to represent the bread, which we later converted to a line showing the distance between two points representing distance, time, or velocity in problems found in the Olivotto's arithmetic collection.

In Romania, in general there was a strong belief that all students could attain and exceed the mediocre expectations set by the Ministry of Education. During all my schooling in Romania, high expectations were everywhere in all subjects. I recall in high school (National College Ion Luca Caragiale in Bucharest, Romania) that once we applied and took the entry-level examinations for ninth grade (Romanian language-written and oral examinations, mathematics-written and oral examinations, and history of Romania-written test only), we began our ninth grade in classrooms only for girls or only for boys in a mixed gender high school. The separation was only for one year, and higher results in academics were documented for both gender groups.

Beginning with tenth grade we were placed in a class that would fit our inclination, and I ended up being in an Olympiad Chemistry class with a relatively small group totaling 23 students. Other students opted for the Olympiad Mathematics class, languages, and so on. Other colleagues from my ninth grade group opted for a no-mathematics environment as they did not want to invest the time and effort in succeeding in mathematics and/or sciences because of their other interests in history, theater, drawing, or other areas.

Passive Transfer of Book Knowledge into My Head

One day I was desperate, as I felt totally unprepared for the mathematics test set for the next day. Evening came, and I was still unprepared after playing after school instead of studying. I asked father what he would do if, after studing for a test, he still felt unprepared. He suggested placing the textbook under the pillow to allow knowledge transfer for the whole night. Needless to say that morning came, and I was still unprepared for the test (Figure 2.2). From my father's joke I understood one thing: there was no passive transfer of knowledge.

Figure 2.2. Hedy... preparing for the test.

Building Test Tubes

Being one of the Olympiad Chemistry students in high school means a lot in terms of commitment to learn and succeed. As an unspoken requirement, we (the 23 students in class) need to solve problems from the Olympiad in mathematics and in chemistry, as well as invent new problems, to be accepted by Olympiad journals, published by a group within Romania. Intellectual work goes beyond normal in Olympiad Chemistry, and we learn to work together and focus on some portions of the work while copying the rest if we do not have time to solve it by ourselves.

Chemistry is always taking place in the laboratory, and on days off we go to visit chemical factories, institutions involving chemistry, chemistry research facilities, even laboratories for the dissection of cadavers as some of my fellow students are determined to go to medical school.

One day we go to visit a factory focused on building a variety of chemical apparatuses from test tubes to extremely complex structures needed for the chemical industry. Our teacher decides that we should build our own glass test tubes using glass tubing since we are constantly breaking them in the lab. Each student chooses his or her glass tubing with a certain diameter. Each student is given a work place with special gas connections in order to get the high temperature flame, takes test tube measurements, receives safety instructions and gets dressed for the job. As we begin working, we realize the difference between theoretically building test tubes (in our minds), observing the workers in the factory perform the task (abstract), and actually building a test tube that looks normal and is somewhat functional (concrete). All our test tubes are irregularly elongated at their bottoms, and the finish is far from perfect.

In the test tube stand we each have to fill - 12 total, there are no two test tubes that are alike. Needless to say, none of us advances to building a Buchner flask, a thick-walled, Erlenmeyer flask with a sidearm, made using a narrow glass piece of tubing fused to the flask, for use with holding vacuums.

As a gift, when we are to leave the factory, all the students receive a mini animal made of glass with all the features, built by the glass workers while we were busy trying to make test tubes.

While we did not learn to become factory workers and prepare glass apparatuses, we learned an important lesson in understanding the process of learning science involved in building some of the apparatuses we had taken for granted. That experience taught me to value talent for manual work and the results of such work. Following this experience, all 23 students in class were careful about chemical glass apparatus and the equipment replacement cost dropped dramatically.

Questions Set 2.2:

1. Can you recall a formal situation in which you learned science and/or mathematics? Write one to two paragraphs describing the experience.
2. In small groups discuss some of the characteristics of the experience (concrete and/or abstract, relevance to your life, level of difficulty, creativity involved, etc.).
3. Create a table representing characteristics of successful science and/or mathematics learning experiences for the whole class. Identify and discuss patterns.

WHAT IS INVOLVED IN LEARNING SCIENCE AND MATHEMATICS AND HOW DO WE MEASURE LEARNING?

This section discusses major documents in the area of science and mathematics that are pertinent to how we learn these subjects, in light of the 21st century requirements, and it explores how we measure learning using a variety of strategies (also known as assessments, evaluations, or grading policies).

What Is Involved in Learning Science and Mathematics?

It is quite a task to sift through all the research-based studies and recently published documents to decide about which to mention. I am not going to mention all that I have read, as the reference list would grow exponentially, but I feature ones I consider especially important and fundamental to my view of learning in general, and learning science and mathematics, in particular. The literature that I have chosen to include represents my choices and not necessarily the most popular or most cited works.

Rooted in the constructivist epistemology, the writings of Ernst von Glasersfeld, a great philosopher of our time, who passed away at the age of 93 in November 2010, shaped my view of learning. Fluent in four languages because of his Western European background (German, French, Italian and English), Glasersfeld read extensively many philosophical works in their original language. Grounded in Vico from the 17th century and, more recently with Piaget's work, Glasersfeld explored the process of learning and the meaning of knowing. As a result of his deliberations he developed the epistemological wing of constructivism called "radical" constructivism. According to this theory, knowledge does not exist in objects such as books or professors' lectures and notes. Rather, cognizing beings (*Homo sapiens*) construct knowledge when trying to accommodate new information into personal schemata (Glasersfeld, 1988, 1991a, 1991b; Glasersfeld & Cobb, 1983). "Knowledge" and the process of cognizing are therefore seen as inseparable. They reciprocally entail one another in the same way as drawing a "figure" entails categorizing the sheet of paper as "ground" (Glasersfeld & Cobb, 1983, p. 6). In other words, knowledge production is seen only as the result of an active process of making sense and it is personal to the specific cognizing being who produces it. Knowledge cannot be transferred from one to another cognizing being, it can, however, be produced through active thinking.

I was lucky enough to know Glasersfeld personally when he came to Florida State University as a consultant at Ken Tobin's invitation (then my PhD major professor). While I drove Glasersfeld to the research schools in Tallahassee to meet and talk with teachers and visit their classrooms, we talked about radical constructivism and its application in our search to understand and function in our worlds. His enthusiasm, intelligence, vast background knowledge, and his willingness to learn from and with others will remain with me for all of my life. In my eyes, he represented the model of the scholar who knew enough to be considered an expert in his field, while at the same time he was a learner and understood how much there was still to explore and to know (from this, one can see his modesty).

Building on Glasersfeld's writings and talks on radical constructivism, and after the entry of Vygotskyan works into the educational field (1978), many scholars developed other facets of constructivism such as social constructivism (also influenced by other researchers, such as Rogoff & Lave, 1984; Wertsch, 1985), which emphasized the social aspect of learning (Bauersfeld, 1988; Gergen, 1995; Tobin, 1993b). Cobern (1993) conceptualized another facet called contextual or cultural constructivism that focuses on the interaction of subjects with their environment. Taylor (1996) developed the area of critical constructivism that focuses on critical analyses of interactions leading to learning and changing the dynamics to enhance learning. Rodriguez (1998) focused on sociotransformative constructivism by emphasizing the effect of cultures and taking action on learning environments.

Though there are different facets of constructivism, some ideas that hold them together include: 1) knowledge is actively produced by cognizing beings and cannot be transmitted passively; 2) learning can be triggered by an experience that does not accommodate, meaning the individual needs to recognize the cognitive dissonance leading to disequilibrium and choose to learn; and, 3) while we have access to reality, we cannot reproduce it in any way because our minds interpret the reality we are able to perceive and as such provide us with our own reflective version of our own reality.

I agree with researchers who detail the thinking processes during early childhood years and emphasize the importance of other persons (all ages) as well as objects (e.g., toys, kitchen tools, books) and their roles to focus and challenge the young child's thinking process (Bransford, Brown, & Cocking, 2000; Enfield, 2010; Sarason, 2004). Bransford et al. (2000) in their research-based work entitled *How People Learn: Brain, Mind, Experience, and School* emphasize the role of challenging, complex environments that are necessary for animal learning, as expressed through an increased number of synapses and an increased vascularization (blood vessel formation) in the brain. In all successful learning situations, the learner develops her thinking based on what she already knows while problem-solving or performing inquiries and moving from the stage of novice learner into the competent, expert learner. Metacognition helps learning become more productive by identifying patterns leading to better learning and successes in specific learners.

Criteria for Evaluation of Middle School Science Curriculum

With the purpose to "estimate how well material addresses targeted benchmarks from the perspective of what is known about student learning and effective teaching," the American Association for the Advancement of Science (AAAS, 1998, para 19; also AAAS, 2012, para 19) lists seven criteria clusters for evaluation of middle school science textbooks and curricula: 1) providing a sense of purpose, 2) taking account of student ideas, 3) engaging students with phenomena, 4) developing and using scientific ideas, 5) promoting student reflection, 6) assessing progress, and 7) enhancing the learning environment. Basically, evaluators use these seven criteria to assess curricula either across all science benchmarks or just to the benchmarks addressed, to determine the strength and weaknesses for the benchmarks evaluated.

The National Research Council (NRC, 2001, p. 5) defines mathematical proficiency with five strands: 1) conceptual understanding, 2) procedural fluency, 3) strategic competence, 4) adaptive reasoning, and 5) productive disposition. It shows these five strands intertwined in a braid, so all five strands are necessary for proficiency in mathematics. These five strands have served as the foundation for mathematics curriculum reform and conceptualization of more specific principles for mathematics learning, such as those proposed by Fuson, Kalchman, and Bransford (2005). Fuson et al. (2005) delineate the principles for learning mathematics: 1) teachers must engage students' preconceptions, 2) understanding requires factual knowledge and conceptual frameworks, and 3) metacognitive approach enables student self-monitoring. To help students address any preconceptions of mathematics, teachers want students to learn that mathematics is about "solving important and relevant quantitative problems" (p. 223), not about computations and following rules. Teachers can encourage students to develop multiple pathways to solve problems and to develop "math talk." Teachers can encourage their mathematics students to develop "conceptual understanding and procedural fluency, as well as an effective organization of knowledge" (p. 231). From the metacognition principle, teachers want to encourage each students to be "a learner, a thinker, and problem solver" (p. 236)—if students do not develop this way of thinking, they may, for the rest of their lives, think of themselves as non-mathematical, which would influence them greatly.

The NRC (2005) book, *How Students Learn: History, Mathematics, and Science in the Classroom*, summarizes four aspects of the classroom environment: 1) learner-centered lens, 2) knowledge-centered lens, 3) assessment-centered lens, and 4) community-centered lens (in which the other three lenses are immersed). These aspects are all present whether the student is learning science, mathematics, history, or any subject.

In science, in a chapter in this NRC book, Donovan and Bransford (2005c) suggest similar findings with learning mathematics, and outline three principles in teaching science: 1) addressing students' preconceptions, 2) knowledge of what it means to 'do science', and 3) metacognition. Prior experiences influence students in their learning and attitudes towards science, so it is critical to start by engaging students in discussion to learn "what they know or how they know it" (Bransford & Donovan, 2005, p. 414) before starting to teach new science material.

Inquiry teaching and teaching habits of mind are critical too to engage students in doing science, not just learning results obtained and reported in their textbook. Teachers want to

> ...help students develop the habits of mind to reflect spontaneously on their own thinking and problem solving, to encourage them to activate relevant background knowledge and monitor their understanding, and to support them in trying the lens through which those in a particular discipline view the world. (Bransford & Donovan, 2005, p. 21)

In short, teachers can (and should) encourage their students to engage in discussions as they develop a "learning community" while exchanging ideas and listening to one another.

The book, *Understanding by Design* (Wiggins & McTighe, 1998), explores the different facets of human learning (or understanding). A learner: 1) can explain (more like a summary), 2) can interpret, 3) can apply, 4) has perspective (awareness of personal/others' perspectives), 5) can empathize (even when different from personal understanding), and 6) has self-knowledge (awareness of personal biases and limitations). The authors suggest having learners experience the six different levels of understanding.

Tobias fights her discomfort with mathematics (1980, 1987) and science (1992; see also Tobias & Tomizuka, 1992) by writing extensively about overcoming or avoiding the science/mathematics psychological blocks (or phobias – also addressed by Mallow, 1978, 1981, 1986). All these texts support the idea that although mathematics and science are interesting, dynamic, and challenging—attributes that would invite humans into exploring these subjects—these subjects are taught in a way that contradicts what we know about human learning (Bransford et al., 2000; Enfield, 2010; Sarason, 2004).

Homo sapiens' Potential for Learning

As a last point in the discussion on learning, I need to introduce the subject of the evolution of the species of *Homo sapiens* or the knowing/wise/thinking man/human from Africa about 200,000 years ago (O'Neill, 2010; Smithsonian National Museum of National History, 2010) after a period of rapid brain expansion. I will not elaborate on isotopic dating and analysis of various fossils found all over the globe from before and after this date, as this is not the focus of this book. It is enough to report that a Google search yielded over four million hits on *Homo sapiens* and the number grows exponentially. It is important to underline *Homo sapiens'* potential for learning (thinking, knowing, and becoming wise). Human ability to learn is not only the result of brain expansion, provided to us with this learning potential 200,000 years ago, but also the ability to continue to build synapses and elongated dendrites by using the available material for processing/thinking/learning. McCrone (1992) suggests that the development of language contributes to the ability of today's *Homo sapiens* to reach such a developed level of thinking, which is superior to all the other organisms in the animal kingdom. Our complex social structures, ability to influence learning for new generations, use of fire to cook our food and the ability to clothe our bodies are unique to humans.

Ken Tobin, a global figure in science education, in an interview with Siry (2009) states: "I think if you are alive, you are learning" (p. 203). Of course, he is "thinking," meaning processing information, or learning. As we all have the potential by birth (*Homo sapiens*), we choose to engage in thinking and problem-solving in order to learn.

Questions Set 2.3:

1. Use literature review on learning and understanding to analyze examples used for with the first question in Questions Set 2.2 (p. 24). What important aspects of learning and understanding science and mathematics were there? What was missing?
2. Use pair-share to determine and discuss class patterns for good experiences and for bad experiences.

How Do We Measure Learning?

With learning there is an inherent need to be able to constantly measure what was learned in order to know the steps to proceed. Unfortunately, no instrument like a "learning meter" (Figure 2-3), measuring in some unit in the International System of Units, exists.

Because of this lack of objectivity, we are left to design different systems for assessing/evaluating/grading students' knowledge and to use a wide range of techniques to determine learning gains. In this section I elaborate on how I see the differences among assessment, evaluation, and grading, their subjective nature, and ways we use them.

Assessment is the process of collecting information about a student. It includes, but is not restricted to, performance on tests, quizzes, projects, laboratory work, in-class and out-of-class group participation, homework and classwork assignments, parental support and attitudes, and relations with siblings. The collection process of assessment is very subjective, as I (as an example of a person) tend to see only things that make sense to me but not to others.

Evaluation means the process of selecting various items/entries collected during the assessment process and assigning them value: e-valu(e)-ation. As I am the person doing the selecting and the person allocating the percentage, I find that the process of evaluation is also subjective, meaning the evaluation depends on the person making the decisions.

Figure 2.3. The Learning Meter.

Grading is the process of transforming the different items that were evaluated into an average percentage or number range (e.g., in Romania school, grades extend from grades 1-10, in Russia from 1-5, in Australia from BAND 1-6,) or letters representing ranges (e.g., in the USA with grades from A, the highest, to F, meaning failure). Some institutions such as Evergreen State College in Olympia, Washington discontinued using numbers and letters, and instead report student learning and academic progress using narratives from teachers and students (self-evaluations) (The Evergreen State College, 2010). Despite the willingness to create universal systems that transfer the average percentage resulting from the evaluation into grades, these transfers are very much influenced by teachers' goals and preferences. As an example, a science teacher in an elite high school decides to combine students' "C" averages with the "B" averages into the "B" grade category in order to lower the number of students who do not pass his class. Some institutions in the USA use either a minus or a plus in addition to the letter grade (e.g., B^+ or B^-), while others do not. Because of the variety of practices used to translate evaluation results into final grades, I find grading to be also a subjective process. In summary, current-day assessment (collecting student data information), evaluation (selecting assessed items and allocating points/percentages), and grading (calculating averages and providing the final grade) make measuring learning a subjective process.

Literature on the process of assessment, evaluation and grading fills numerous books and research articles. Distinctions are made among the following categories of assessment strategies to find information on student knowledge on a subject at a certain point in time:

1. Formative assessment: on going, relatively short (one to four questions). Usually in the range of giving students a few minutes to respond, used to inform instruction on a continuous basis.
2. Summative assessment: at the end of a chapter, small unit, middle of the semester, or at the end of a semester. Students are provided ample time to respond to a variety of questions, asking for answer selection (e.g., multiple choice), matching items, short answer or elaborated constructed response, or portfolio (i.e., identifying a goal, number of items to be included, and a reflection discussing the items in terms of goal and improvement), used to determine extent of knowledge on a curricular topic.
3. Diagnostic assessment: verbal and/or written, usually short, used to inform instruction by uncovering students' knowledge prior to teaching; also used to identify misconceptions that need to be challenged during instruction.
4. Formal assessment: usually announced and with handouts. Example: summative assessment.
5. Informal assessment: done at different points during the lesson or afterward, usually done verbally with a few students in class or via observations (e.g., with laboratory work). Example: formative assessment.

6. Traditional assessment: in the USA refers to answering multiple-choice and/or matching items on tests. In other countries (e.g., Armenia, Romania, Israel) involves open-ended questions on tests.

7. Alternative: in the USA, alternative refers to anything other than traditional assessment (Moscovici & Gilmer, 1996; Tchudi & Lafer, 1996) and includes projects, performances during laboratory inquiries or the laboratory report, responses to open-ended questions, portfolios, student performances, and even addition of a short explanation/reasoning for the selected choice made on a multiple-choice question. Participation in Trends in International Mathematics and Science Study (TIMSS) (and later, Programme for International Student Assessment, PISA) has forced many countries that did not use multiple-choice questions in schools to begin using these item formats in order to familiarize students and help them succeed with this type of questioning.

8. Teacher/self/peer assessment: different individuals performing an analysis of learned material. Successful programs use these different perspectives during a reflective session to focus on improving the quality of the experience for all involved.

9. Reflective assessment (Daniels & Bizar, 2005): used as a feedback mechanism for all involved in an effort to improve teaching and learning experiences.

10. Authentic assessment: used to assess understanding and knowledge gained in a real-life situation.

11. Performance assessment: task completion, such as preparing a slide for the microscope or preparing a skit to demonstrate the use of fractions in mathematics.

12. High cognitive demand assessment: student performance with respect to synthesis, analysis, evaluation, and/or application of knowledge gained to create new situations (Bloom, Hastings, & Madaus, 1971; Chiu, 2009; Stein, Smith, & Silver, 1999; Zoller, 2001).

13. Low cognitive demand assessment: student-recall usually "isolatable bits of information" (Bloom et al., 1971, p. 271), comprehension (student knows what is communicated) via translation (from one language to another), interpretation (including new organization/personal lens), or extrapolation (expanding beyond given dataset, using the same given abstraction/pattern), and application (using abstractions, in particular, and concrete examples).

14. Verbal (oral) and/or written assessments: assessments emphasizing the ability of students to verbalize their knowledge and/or rely on ability to write well.

15. Timed as opposed to ample time to respond assessment: timed testing is used for most school-based performance measures in the USA. The intent is to introduce the competitive angle because there might not be enough time to complete the testing, even in the case of gifted students (normal curve expectations) (Tsui & Mazzocco, 2007).

The list of terms grows the more we read. Longitudinal assessment (Wiggins & McTighe, 1998) looks at collecting data on continuous progressions of understanding with recurring tasks. While still debatable, value-added analysis of student data looks at contributions made by specific teachers, for example, over middle school years (Amrein-Beardsley, 2008).

Returning to the subject of demonstrating student learning of science and mathematics (Donovan & Bransford, 2005b), with the ample list of assessment strategies listed above, we have a clearer vision as to the need for cohesiveness among goals for learning/understanding in terms of levels of cognition, the way science and mathematics teachers should teach (in Chapter 4), and the way we should assess our students or finding the knowledge that really counts.

Looking at the assessment systems for standardized testing in the USA, Daniels and Bizar (2005) are teachers who are "receiving a schizophrenic message: teach in creative, innovative, constructive ways, but your students will be tested very differently" (p. 225). In the USA the standardized testing system (for example Standardized Testing and Reporting – STAR for schools in California, Advanced Placement (AP) examinations during high school years, even Scholastic Aptitude Test (SAT) examinations necessary for applying for admission to higher education in the USA focus on disconnected pieces of information requiring low level cognitive skills. Parallel with a destructive standardized assessment system, teachers are educated to teach using various methodologies, assess students using a variety of strategies, provide continuous feedback for student improvement, and focus on developing and assessing students' higher cognitive skills. The disconnection between teaching methodologies and assessment in the USA results in confusion, not only for teachers and students, but also for the broader communities in which schools are situated.

Questions Set 2.4:

1. Looking at assessment strategies, which ones did you experience as a student learning science and or mathematics? As a teacher? Which ones fit your learning style?
2. Connect your answers to Question # 1 above to the answers to your first question in Question Sets 2.2 (p. 24) and Question Sets 2.3 (p. 28) (in two to three paragraphs on a learning experience and inclusion of learning principles from the literature review on learning - refer to pages 24 and 28).
3. Design an assessment that you would like to see for a science and/or mathematics class in which you participate as a student or as the teacher.
4. Compare/contrast assessments developed in terms of goals, expressing learning, cognitive levels, requirements for teaching strategies, and describe patterns found in the literature pertinent to learning and assessing.

SO, WHAT DOES IT MEAN TO KNOW SCIENCE AND MATHEMATICS?

As previously mentioned in this chapter, the meaning of knowing science and mathematics is the ability of individuals to engage in learning these subjects in specific contexts and in using the assessment system that collects information pertaining to learned material. Cohesiveness between learning and assessing in science and mathematics is a must (Daniels & Bizar, 2005).

In the following paragraphs I underline the characteristics of the learning experiences in science and mathematics that have high potential in terms of learning (Glasersfeld, 1988; Tobin, 1993b; Zoller, 2001).

Relevance and Involvement

I began this chapter by showing the role of previous knowledge and the relevance of the topic in determining individual's choice to get involved in learning. As I was enjoying myself in the Black Sea waters during my childhood years I learned about waves and flux/reflux movement of the sea. Proportions came easily to me because I was practicing the concept using division of candies and even irregular pieces of transparent sugar with my cousin who was older and thought he could cheat me.

Involvement in science and mathematics begins during early childhood years when children lack the "syntax;" however, they are still able to express learning through facial expressions and movements.

Looking at the literature on learning and knowing (Glasersfeld, 1988), it seems that learning is based on what one knows and is the result of disequilibrium or new information contradicting previous knowledge/schema. In a way, this theory expects the learner to get involved in learning or choose to disregard the challenge. For example, I gave up becoming a test tube producer after trying to create them during my high school experience. Test tube production was relevant; however, I decided not to get involved in performing the techniques any longer, as it was cheaper for me to purchase ones already made.

Challenging/High Expectations

Learning happens when the task/experience is challenging enough to support curiosity and learning (Glasersfeld, 1988); however if specific learning is expected, the challenge level needs to be lower than the breaking point, or the point when the individual decides to quit. The fact that the task is challenging needs to be combined with having high expectations of the individuals involved in solving the challenge in ways that would show appropriate use of higher order cognitive/thinking skills (Zoller, 2001). Looking back at the fraction example using the loaf of bread, Ms. Bayer expected all students in class to be able to divide the two bread halves, into equal thirds. She always used real-life word problems to initiate learning of a new concept and to develop first our conceptual understanding of the problem at hand. Lots of guiding questions helped us identify what was known and what we needed to find out. Once the conceptual understanding was mastered, Ms. Bayer used numerical exercises to help perfect the procedural part of solving these kinds of numerical exercises (Donovan & Bransford, 2005b).

Time to Think and Process/Re-process Information

In order to facilitate learning of science and mathematics, individuals need to have ample time to think and rethink/process information, identify variables, pose alternative solutions, etc. On many occasions, time restrictions result in task modification and students' learning is restricted (Moscovici, 2002b). An excellent technique to avoid restricted learning is Think-Pair-Share, in which individuals first design and record ways (think) to solve a problem,[2] then discuss (pair/share) alternatives coming from different individuals/groups. After understanding others' approaches to the same problem, individuals should choose the best or most effective way to solve the problem (Wiggins & McTighe, 1998). Some individuals might need time to discuss and clarify verbally the challenge/problem before attempting to solve it individually.

Autonomy

Individuals involved in science and mathematics learning need to be supported in their belief that they have a say in the process of finding a solution to the problem presented, and the ability to explain/defend their answer (Tobin, 1991). They should have the right to ask for clarifications without fearing disrespect from the teacher or their classmates. Participants should be encouraged to challenge each other's solutions, propose new ones, as well as decide on tasks/experiences that have the potential of enhancing the learning partnership situation.

Looking back at my experience with Ms. Bayer, I realize that she used students in class to clarify what is known in the problem and what we needed to find. We determined what we were going to find. I recall one of the Olivotto arithmetic problems, which asked for the time to fill a pool when two faucets were opened at different times. Ms. Bayer drew the pool on the blackboard and asked us where to place faucets, where to write given information, and to define the beginning times. Her tone following student's answer was of questioning, "really?" and turning to the whole class "what do you think?" Ms Bayer and most of my teachers during my education in Romania showed respect for students' supported opinions and always pushed for more, expecting better from us.

Commitment

We can create all the conditions possible for successful science and mathematics learning; however, the ultimate decision to accept the challenge and get involved in the science inquiry or mathematics problem-solving remains with the learner.

As we tend to say, "We can bring the horse to the water, but we cannot make it drink." Learners need to understand their choices and focus on long-term learning that ensures building thinking capacity of *Homo sapiens*. Contributing to a learner's decision not to engage in learning might be a variety of factors, such as talk that is too difficult and not comprehensible, no support from classmates or from teachers, disrespectful climate, task not challenging enough, low expectations, not enough time to engage in the task, lack of voice in the process of learning, lack of task relevance, or disregard for the assessment results.

On numerous occasions I experienced lack of personal commitment when I had to memorize terms or dates, just to "succeed" on a test. I recall the assessment on human anatomy – the skeleton – sometime in seventh or eighth grade when we had to associate the names of bones with their locations in the skeleton. I do not recall the grade, however, the fact is that I never took another anatomy class in my life as a biologist if I knew that I would have to just memorize information. In addition to my dislike of anatomy, this recall for class assessment proved useless in the long run, as I never used these anatomical terms in my various careers, nor do I recall any of the ones memorized just for the test.

Aligning Learning Expectations, Assessment Strategies, and Teaching

One of the most difficult tasks for teachers in California is to correlate standards that are written as "students will know" or "students will understand" in state documents without specifying the way that the students will demonstrate their knowledge or understanding (California Department of Education, 1998). As such, defining learning objectives in terms of possible assessment strategies proves to be a difficult task.

The National Council for Teachers of Mathematics published a landmark book, *Principles and Standards for School Mathematics* (NCTM, 2000). In 2012, the NCTM updated its vision of the teaching of mathematics:

> *Principles and Standards for School Mathematics* describes a future in which all students have access to rigorous, high-quality mathematics instruction, including four years of high school mathematics. Knowledgeable teachers have adequate support and ongoing access to professional development. The curriculum is mathematically rich, providing students with opportunities to learn important mathematical concepts and procedures with understanding. Students have access to technologies that broaden and deepen their understanding of mathematics. More students pursue educational paths that prepare them for lifelong work as mathematicians, statisticians, engineers, and scientists. (NCTM, 2012)

The NRC (2011) worked with the NSTA to develop a framework for K-12 science education, which includes practices, crosscutting concepts, and the core ideas of science and engineering. This framework lays the foundation for the next generation of science education K-12 standards, still to be developed. Once the new standards are developed, another NRC committee will develop the assessments to go with the framework and these new national standards, which hopefully will be internally consistent, build on each other, be used throughout the USA in K-12 education, and be modified for other countries and cultures.

NOTES

[2] Called T-P-S, for think, pair, share. Retrieved from http://serc.carleton.edu/introgeo/interactive/ tpshare.html

EMOTIONAL AND INTELLECTUAL INVOLVEMENT WHILE LEARNING SCIENCE AND MATHEMATICS

INTRODUCTION

This chapter considers the relationship between cognition and emotion associated with learning science and mathematics and addresses how and why one might choose different learning pathways when facing challenges involving these subjects. As you may know, disequilibrium, belly ache/arousal and pleasure are not only strong responses but each is also associated with successful learning. In terms of biological changes, new protein synthesis and the creation of neural networks are known processes that occur during meaningful learning. Not unsurprising, education (and/or learning) is a recipe for slowing down or even stopping some forms of dementia, even Alzheimer's disease. In order to have successful learning (i.e., facing a challenge), the learner needs to achieve a balance between potentially negative emotions (i.e., fear, anxiety, sadness) and positive emotions (e.g., happiness, pleasure, enjoyment).

BEFORE SCHOOL ERA – FOCUS ON EARLY CHILDHOOD EDUCATION

I think I have learned an enormous amount in my squads even though I don't necessarily come with the intention of learning something, and I might not even enjoy the process of learning something new, because often times learning something new necessitates changes in direction when you were perfectly happy with the way you were going. (Ken Tobin quoted interview in Siry, 2009, p. 203)

It is a well-known fact that our natural curiosity and our minds' tendency to continue thinking lead us into learning situations. We bring to our consciousness unsolved situations that need resolving or solved situations that need rethinking or re-challenging, so decisions can be modified or changed. We tend to prioritize decisions about what needs to be solved immediately and what can wait because we are incapable of focusing on all unsolved issues in our lives simultaneously.

We are also aware that an orchestra of emotions performs in concert with the reasoning processes as we consciously address data sources and reason with alternatives. While Bloom et al. (1971) discuss the importance of cognitive and affective objectives, which can also be considered different domains of knowledge, schooling tends to evaluate the cognitive objectives (domain) and disregard the affective domain.

Playing "Sus-Jos" ["Up-Down" in Translation – Similar to
"Chutes and Ladders" Game]

The Sus-Jos board game is played on a colored and animated game board with a train of connecting squares determining advancement during the game. One's starting move and advancement are usually dependent on throwing a die and counting off the value on the upper side of the die. At different locations (squares) on the board, the player needs to conform to additional requirements, such as "go back to the beginning" or "move pawn five places forward." The game has many alternatives such as throwing a pair of dice and using the result of subtraction or addition of the two die values. Differently colored pawns allow up to six players at one time, or in the case of three players, each player using two different pawns. In the game below played by Elena, Peter, John, and me, a value of six on one of the die was required to start the game. The added value of the two die represented the number of places one was allowed to move.

I recall discussions that focused on my attempts to use any advantage to avoid traps and negative squares and win. Here is an example:

Elena: [looking at the square asking to begin from the beginning]: 5+6= 13. I should be getting here [placing her pawn 2 spaces after the square for 11 spaces that required the player to begin at the start].

Hedy: [using her fingers]: No way! It cannot be more than 12!

Peter: Why?

John: Elena knows to add!

Hedy [after adding using her fingers]: It is 11 – [looking at Elena] you need to do it again!

Peter: Hedy is right!

Elena [showing surprise that she messed up on such a simple addition exercise]: Oops! Hedy is right – sorry! I jumped too fast!

Sometimes we made rules during the game, such as separating the values of the dice and making sure that each value was considered separately, or just using the combined values of the die. Issues would arise when one of the players might have an advantage from a rule, or the rule might prove to be disadvantageous to a competitor.

Sus-Jos proved to be a great incentive for learning addition (or subtraction) based on counting and translating die values from a picture of dots into places (squares) on a game board, performing mental mathematics and working on shortening processing time, and trying to cheat. Slowly, cheating became impossible as our skills improved. The game also shed light on assessing personal and others' abilities for mental addition. As we were using different scaffolds to perform the exercises at a fast pace, one had to be open to understanding other ways to add (knowing the maximum for two dice as 12, or using addition on our fingers to perform (5)+(5+1)). During the Sus-Jos game, emotions were high. We felt anxiety as our turn came for fear of getting a combination that would place our pawn in a square requiring us to go backspaces. Game play was also full of positive emotion, when the dice values proved advantageous to us, or disadvantageous to a competitor. The ability to engage in fast mental mathematics also added to the tension.

Playing "Tarile" [Pronounced "Tzarile" – Meaning "Countries"]

"Tarile" was a very popular game in the 1970s in Romania (Arsenie & Dan, 2009). The game involved a medium-large ball (volleyball/basketball) and two concentric circles. The circle with the smaller radius represented the space where one could throw the ball in the air, and the circle with the larger radius represented the space where one could run. As we grew older, the larger circle was eliminated in our game and one had to be far enough away not to get hit; however, close enough to be able to catch a ball after it was thrown in the air. Children of different ages could participate. Each would select a country. The person with the ball would simultaneously throw the ball in the air and call a country name. The child whose country was called was supposed to catch the ball before it hit the ground, throw it in the air while standing in the smaller circle and name another country. If the catcher did not catch the ball, her only way to remain in the game would be to hit another child with the ball with that child not catching it. Children had to stop running once the ball was in a child's hands. Very quickly we (children) learned to throw the ball in the air to a low height if we called a country where the catcher was far. We would run immediately, as the chances were that the ball would hit the ground before the catcher could get it. Variables such as running ability, ability to control the height of the ball in the air, ability to throw the ball perpendicular to the earth's surface (curved throws were not allowed), ability to stop, turn, and run in the opposite direction, ability to avoid bumping into other children while running and recording who they were, were involved in successful play.

Emotions ran high in this game too. The multiple variables involved muddied the solutions for the perfect game. Knowing my abilities and evaluating the advantages and disadvantages of my friends' game were essential. Still, because the game depended on multiple variables, there was still a high degree of unpredictability with every decision. Fear that while we ran, the catcher would catch the ball and call our country combined with anger that what we predicted actually happened - happiness if we could catch the ball despite the challenge and sadness when our friends were eliminated in the process. Persevering, reassessing situations constantly, and thinking on the spot were just a few skills that developed and improved during these games.

Questions Set 3.1:

1. Do you recall a similar informal experience during your before school age when you experienced high emotional levels while learning science and/or mathematics? Write one to two paragraphs.

2. In small groups discuss similarities and differences between experiences shared and write one to two paragraphs summarizing these. Use graphics if needed.
3. Create a table of experiences for the whole class and connect these to emotions felt during these experiences.

EMOTIONS INVOLVED IN LEARNING SCIENCE AND MATHEMATICS DURING SCHOOLING YEARS

While we continued to play educational games even at school (e.g., paper battleships, dominos, various card games) and experienced similar emotions as the ones described during early childhood years, formal learning added the pressure of recording results and keeping track via grades of successful and unsuccessful events, as defined by the grade received. As a student in Romania reported her grades to her parents on a daily basis (the grade notebook needed parent's signature on the following school day), school events tended to affect the student's life through the parents' responses. However, an unsuccessful playing event outside school could be forgotten, never mentioned again.

School in Romania in the 1960s and 1970s emphasized building students' confidence in subject content at all levels and in different manners: *written* (tests/quizzes), *verbal* (i.e., ability to articulate cohesively the road to finding a solution to a problem while writing on the board or talking aloud, use visuals during presentations, express differences among various ways to solve a problem in full and clear sentences), and *oral* (i.e., thoughts, comparison/contrast of listener's to student presenter's way of solving problems, and ability to articulate differences when asked by the teacher). Grades mirrored the different emphases - we had oral grades (e.g., for presenting our solutions to the class and participating in the discussion on various solutions), as well as grades on written assignments (e.g., individuals tests, homework, projects).

Write a Composition on a Memorable Event that Happened During the Summer Vacation and Draw a Picture

For years in the lower grades I dreaded the assignment of writing a memorable event at the beginning of the academic year - not because I did not have memorable experiences, but as I learned later, because I was not considered a good writer or an artist. My compositions sounded like telegrams of essential facts, and my drawings were a far cry from reality.

Here is an example of an essay on the topic of a vacation with my family at the Black Sea:

We go with my family to Mamaia (a summer vacation city near the Black Sea).

The sun is shining. It is hot. The water is cold. I play with my sister and other children in the water. I eat chocolate ice cream and have a coke. The ice cream is good. I swim with father far away into the sea. It is scary.

The vacation is great. End.

My drawing was also uninspiring. As I could not draw people, I drew skeletal forms (small circle for the head, a larger oval for the body, and lines representing arms and legs) and avoided depicting characters, whenever possible. Animals were also out of the question, and the only dog that I recall ever drawing was based on a picture, and the teacher thought it was a donkey! The blue sky, the large yellow beach, and the dark blue sea helped me fill large areas of the drawing. As I lacked technical drawing skill, even the large spots of color were more like random lines of color using different angles and directions, without shadows and lighting.

Despite the mostly positive emotions connected to the actual vacation experience, an amalgam of negative emotions ran high during my preparation of the assignment as well as during the sharing session. During the sharing session, fellow students who were very talented with writing and/or drawing would read and show their work to the class. Meanwhile, I experienced fear from having a low level product, anxiety from having to share, frustration with my inability to express myself either in writing or by representing my experiences in drawings, and shame that my product did not compare with the exceptional work of many, if not most of my classmates (at least that was the way it looked to me during those days). The teacher would interpret my lack of success as lack of effort, which was not true. I was putting more time into completing this assignment than into solving mathematics problems. Today, with the development of the research literature on multiple intelligences and student dispositions, my unsuccessful efforts to write and draw might have been interpreted differently.

Needless to say that while I was able to talk about ways to solve mathematics problems in detail and describe negative emotions related to these challenges (e.g., anger, frustration, disappointment), I could not transfer these abilities into writing and drawing about summer experiences.

Struggling With Stoichiometry in High School

At the intersection of mathematics, chemistry, and language demands lies the topic of stoichiometry – one of the most difficult topics in what is called "applied" chemistry. With its roots in Greek (*stoicheion* = element and *metron* = measure), the term allows quantification related to chemical reactions and chemical composition. In other words, using the concept of the mole, stoichiometry allows us to calculate the theoretical number of grams needed react one compound or element with another, using specific solutions and processes.

I recall these kinds of examples and the expected transformations from grams to moles and back to grams, using proportions after balancing equations. While I understood each part of the problem process separately, such as the necessity to balance equations, the meaning of a mole, calculation of molecular mass, and use of Avogadro's number representing the number of molecules in one mole of a pure substance (or number of atoms in one mole of a pure element), I felt fazed with solving an entire problem. I would experience the "flight or fight" response - the freezing effect paralyzing my brain for the duration of a stoichiometry quiz or test. I remember staring at the blank sheet of paper and having no clue as to figuring out what was being asked, or what slices of knowledge I should use. Conceptually, I did not have a clear picture and procedurally I could only function in disconnected subtasks.

In Romania we did not have multiple-choice questions with four alternatives from which to choose the right answer. Therefore, I could not use any checking techniques to identify a most plausible answer. Sometimes my classmates would help, taking a risk of being caught in the process by telling me how to solve the problem or by giving me the final answer. As teachers requested to see how one got to the answer, only being given the final result was not helpful – it just gave a hint in terms of magnitude and units.

Pain, disappointment in my inability to function in the advanced stoichiometry world, and fear of poor performance in this topic followed me through high school. Note that the discomfort, pain, disappointment, and fear I experienced with my inability to grasp stoichiometry in high school, were directed toward the <u>subject</u> (stoichiometry) and not the <u>teacher(s)</u> who failed to help me learn the subject. I had a great deal of respect and admiration for the teachers of this subject as they tried (unsuccessfully) to help.

Fortunately, I had excellent results in other chemistry topics, mathematics, and other subject areas, as well as in sports, and I was socially accepted and and could organize social events and gatherings. Positive emotions associated with these areas helped me balance negative emotions resulting from my encounters with unsuccessful learning situations, such as in the case of stoichiometry in high school and the "draw and write a composition" during my first to eighth grade experience.

Questions Set 3.2 :

1. Can you recall a formal situation in which you learned science and/or mathematics? Write one to two paragraphs describing the experience (you can use the one described in the first question from Question Set 2.2) (p. 24) and emotions associated with the specific situation.
2. Can you recall a formal situation in which you could not grasp a concept in science and/or mathematics? Describe emotions related to the situation.
3. In small groups discuss emotions related to successful and unsuccessful science and/or mathematics formal learning experiences.
4. Create a table for the whole class representing emotions associated with successful and unsuccessful formal learning situations in science and/or mathematics. Identify and discuss patterns.

EMOTIONS INVOLVED IN LEARNING SCIENCE AND MATHEMATICS

In order to address this subject, first I explore the most extreme cases of dislike or discomfort associated with science and mathematics - the phobias - in light of the accepted U.S. norm of the "normal" (from here the word "norm") citizen neither knowing nor being comfortable with these subjects. Following, I expand on available perspectives and the literature on emotions during learning in general, and during learning science and mathematics in particular. I close by presenting my perspective on the dynamics of emotions when learning science and mathematics, based on my experiences in countries holding very different viewpoints on who should learn, and reasons one should learn, know and be able to use science and mathematics.

Science and Mathematics Phobias

I began researching the concepts of science and mathematics phobias many years ago, because I was trying to understand better ways to prepare the pre-service elementary school teachers who were enrolled in my elementary science mathematics methods courses at an urban university in Southern California, USA. I was able to feel their pain and fear when these subjects were mentioned (I found that just saying "geometry" or "photosynthesis" paralyzed almost all of them and fear would show in their eyes, as well as in their body language). Phobias (i.e., persistent, irrational, and excessive fears) may be the result of classical conditioning, that is the linking of a neutral stimulus with a trauma stimulus, a connection leading to a conditioned phobia (Nevid, Rathus, & Greene, 2003; Oltmanns & Emery, 2003). In the case of my elementary school methods course, my mention the words "geometry," or "stoichiometry" could have triggered students' fear of being called upon, pain from the inability to contribute to the discussion, or sense of failure to understand the concept. Similar to Pavlov's conditioning experiment in which the dog associated the sound of a bell with receiving food (and as such, triggered salivation), each mentioning of the word "geometry," or "stoichiometry" may have triggered an emotional cascade connected to phobia. Individuals suffering from science and/or mathematics phobia avoid these subjects, because they want to avoid the pain and fear triggered when the subjects are mentioned.

On the page where Oltmanns and Emery (2003, p. 193) explain phobias is a Far Side cartoon by Gary Larson entitled, "Math phobic's nightmare." The cartoon shows an angel reading from a book and an adult facing what I imagine to be the entrance to heaven. The angel, after clarifying that "nobody gets in here without answering the following question," begins reading a mathematics (arithmetic/algebra) word problem involving two trains travelling toward one another, which have started moving at different times and have different speeds. At some point during the reading of the word problem, the angel asks the adult if he needs paper. The cartoon is self-explanatory. Boeree (2009b) addresses mathematics phobia as part of neurosis referring to

> …a variety of psychological problems involving persistent experiences of negative affect including anxiety, sadness or depression, anger, irritability, mental confusion, low sense of self-worth, etc., behavioral symptoms such as phobic avoidance, vigilance, impulsive and compulsive acts, lethargy, etc., cognitive problems such as unpleasant or disturbing thoughts, repetition of thoughts and perfectionism, schizoid isolation, socioculturally inappropriate behaviors, etc. (para 76)

Highlighting Alfred Adler's contribution to the field of neurosis, Boeree relates to Adler's treatment of math phobia (most common of inferiority complexes), stating that it could be rooted in a child's inability to multiply seven times eight, could get worse every year, and hit the crisis point with "Algebra" when the real question becomes, "How could you be expected to know what "x" is when you still don't know what seven times eight is?" (Boeree, 1997, para 39).

At this point, I need to clarify that I am discussing the topic of emotions and learning in the context of the U.S. population, as the literature (and sometimes events) cited is from research studies performed in the USA. Research conducted in Spain with pre-service elementary school teachers shows alignment with similar populations in the USA (Brigado, Bermejo, Conde, & Mellado, 2010). For both men and women, negative emotions seem to be associated mainly with learning physics and chemistry in secondary classrooms. The same negative emotions are reported when women are asked to teach these subjects at the elementary school level. This finding suggests that men seem to overcome their negative emotions related to learning these subjects during their secondary education.

In my journey of trying to understand why science learning seems to be so difficult (even more than mathematics in many cases), I encountered Jay Lemke's (1998) chapter, *Multiplying meaning*, in which he makes the argument that science is the result of a multimedia collage:

> Science is not done, is not communicated, through verbal language alone. It *cannot* [italics in text] be. The 'concepts' of science are not solely verbal concepts, though they have verbal components. They are semiotic *hybrids* [italics in text], simultaneously and essentially verbal, mathematical, visual-graphical, and actional-operational. The actional, conversational, and written textual genres of science are historically and presently, fundamentally and irreducibly, *multimedia genres* [italics in text]. To do science, to talk science, to read and write science it is necessary to juggle and combine in various canonical ways verbal discourse, mathematical expression, graphical-visual representation, and motor operations in the world. (p. 87)

The ability of the science learner to become comfortable with the different media necessary for doing, talking, writing and reading science is not enough. The learner needs to reach another level where she juggles and is able to "combine in different ways" these abilities in order to gain and communicate science knowledge. As science requires knowledge of applied mathematics, I understand that it has the potential to distance people from believing that they can learn it.

Lemke (1989, 1990, 1992) argues about the elitist nature of science and scientists, while Tobias (1987) looks at the contradiction between 21st century requirements in terms of mathematics use and knowledge on one side, and the avoidance of mathematics by the public on the other side as "those who fear it don't want to think about it; those who escape from school without it don't want to talk about it; and those who practice it don't want to discuss it in public" (p. xvii).

In the case of U.S. culture, I am even more concerned about a newly defined "norm" or what "normal" means in terms of aptitude for science and mathematics. According to Holton (1994), not understanding science is accepted as a "norm" in the general public, even in academia, and in the USA I have even heard expressions such as "It is not only I who don't have an understanding of science.

My parents do not understand it either," implying some kind of inheritance pattern for the "not understanding science gene" (Figure 3.1).

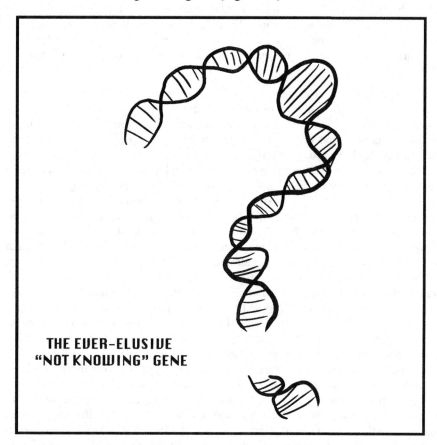

**THE EVER-ELUSIVE
"NOT KNOWING" GENE**

Figure 3.1. The "not understanding" gene.

Two schools appear to be defining the neuroscientific disability to do mathematics – one school looks at brain injuries in adults and correlates these injuries to subjects' inability to do mathematics, while the other school looks at children with no known history of brain injuries (Byrnes, 2008). Byrnes is tentative in summarizing data that connect areas of the brain with mathematical abilities, such as 1) calculation skills (largely confined to the left hemisphere), 2) individual mathematics facts and procedures (stored separately in different areas of the cortex), and 3) ordinality (i.e., ordering of numbers) and comparison skills (mostly in the posterior region of right hemisphere), and the finding that gifted children have more allergies and engage their right hemisphere more often than non-gifted children. Referring to mathematics, Smith (2002) states:

Mathematics isn't in your genes, nor is it wired in your brain cells; it hasn't been around long enough in human history. We can't get mathematics from another person in a transfusion. Mathematics is a combination of human discovery and human invention. If we can learn anything, we can learn mathematics. Whether we want to learn, or think we can learn, is another matter. Anyone can learn negative attitudes. Anyone can learn phobias. (p. 125)

Tsui and Mazzocco's (2007) preliminary study of gifted students' performance on timed tests suggests that a timed test setting has a negative effect on the performances of perfectionist sixth grade mathematics gifted students. When the testing scenario is that of an untimed test following a timed test, the results are statistically significant for girls only.

Other "norms" in the American culture promoted by television and other media include: females being pretty and sexy (washing their hair, having the "right" clothes) making suggestive sex-related movements); females using cleaners and appliances for cleaning their house (e.g., Mr. Clean); females being successful nurses or paralegals who tend to study in their pajamas at on-line universities, while males studying to become electricians or mechanics at Information Technology (IT) Institutes; and, females being expected to take care of the children in the family and sometimes stay home in order to better perform their expected duties. While I understand the differences between males and females in terms of average physical abilities during different age segments, there is no biological indication of differences in their abilities to study a subject such as science or mathematics, and/or to pursue a career in engineering, medicine, or mechanics. Norms and roles are sociocultural constructs with media promoting and sustaining these relations. In order to change the sociocultural norms I have highlighted, we need to promote the beauty of female's internal features, such as intelligence, ability to problem-solve, and ability and success with science and mathematics learning and careers. We need to remember that we are not competing – males against females - but collaborating to change norms (e.g., girls are not good in science and mathematics) that do not contribute to the success of people living in the USA.

The norm of science and mathematics phobias in the general U.S. population might imply that the "norm" evolved as a protection mechanism to guard one's ego from harm. Unfortunately, this science and mathematics phobic "norm" does not help U.S. children to become the global citizen for the 21st century.

Based on his work in the 1970s when he developed a "clinic" at Loyola University in Chicago for treating science anxiety, Mallow (1978, 1981, 1986) writes extensively on science phobia (or fear of science/science anxiety). A physics professor at that time, he wanted to increase the number of physics majors and science majors in general. The clinic used two co-instructors of opposite gender, one with expertise in the science area and the other with expertise in psychology, who taught ten students at a time for seven sessions. Students were co-enrolled in a regular science course. Using a 44-item Science Anxiety Questionnaire, Mallow (1986) reports that "all the students who went through the Clinic showed significant anxiety reduction, compared to a control group who had applied to the Clinic but whose schedules made it infeasible for us to accommodate them" (p. 61). Desensitization (recommended for treating phobias) and active science teaching learning strategies were used in the clinics and results were overwhelmingly positive. In a similar effort to reduce science anxiety and support science students during their studies, Montgomery Community College developed a Science Learning Center (Keyser, 1993). Less formal treatment of science phobia/anxiety was reported for science methods courses (Ramsey-Gassert & Shroyer, 1992), in-service institutes (Cox & Carpenter, 1989), as well as college science classes (Ryan, 1989).

Many biology majors who finish undergraduate and graduate degrees in the area of biology recall negative feelings and emotions during their studies (Herreid, 2001). Herreid focuses on American college science education that was "crippling," but my college science undergraduate education in Israel was similar: "disabling," "debilitating," and "hurtful." While Herreid identifies the source of the negative experiences during undergraduate science as the traditional teaching approach with multiple-choice questions on exams, I can say that the open-response assessment strategies in Israel did not improve my science education experience. Personally, I think that the source of the problem is an elitist feeling held by college science professors whose class test averages are C or lower, and/or in whose classes there is a high failure rate. These professors accept that not all students can master the material to the same level, and they do not seek ways to make science accessible and understandable to more students. Most research universities do not reward professors for good teaching; instead they reward excellent research. Teaching is often viewed as a chore or a service, not an endeavor in which to excel.

Emotions in Learning Science and Mathematics

Because of their overwhelming presence in the "normal" population, I discussed the topic of science and mathematics phobias separately in the previous paragraphs. Now, I explore the literature on the basic emotions: meanings, pathways, and importance in terms of learning, in general, and of learning science and mathematics, in particular.

Basic Emotions

I can truthfully say that I felt overwhelmed trying to understand the meaning of emotions as they relate to learning of science and mathematics. Researchers and theorists from a variety of fields such as sociology, biology (e.g., evolutionary, physiology), anthropology, psychology, psychiatry, education, and neuroscience as well as interdisciplinary fields have written extensively on this subject. Ortony and Turner (1990) and Turner and Ortony (1992) attempt to synthesize major works in these fields and to identify the meaning of the "basicness" (Ortony & Turner, 1990, p. 329) of emotions, only to decide that this "basicness" requires a biological basis and a "hardwired" (p. 324) pathway as the response. Izard (1992) proposes a model to explain emotions as a function of emotion-cognition interactions resulting in affective-cognitive structures. In some cases, noncognitive pathways such as hormonal changes activate emotions, thus the relationship between cognition and emotion is not clear. Izard explains the affective-cognitive appearance of the "social smile" (p. 564) that acknowledges the three weeks infant's perception of the contour of a face; an emotion that later with the development of cognitive functions transforms into joy, becoming even later with verbal representation the "complex affective-cognitive network called *love* [italics in text], a network of feelings, memories and anticipations that are activated by an image of a beloved mother's face" (p. 564). LeDoux, a researcher who began his study of the emotional brain in the mid 1970s by studying patients who had undergone split-brain surgeries (including the cutting of the nerves connecting the left brain hemisphere to the right counterpart), also views emotions as "biological functions of the nervous system. I believe that figuring out how emotions are represented in the brain can help us understand them" (1996, p. 12). While he recognizes the instinctive part of displaying emotions through facial expressions, LeDoux highlights research (e.g., Ekman's experiment comparing Westerners to Orientals in LeDoux, 1996, p. 118; Ekman, 1999) documenting that rules of social display are part of one's socialization process that might restrict individuals from publicly expressing emotions in their facial expressions. In an effort to summarize the transformation from an emotional reaction to conscious emotional experience, LeDoux states:

> We've got a specialized emotion system that receives sensory inputs and produces behavioral, autonomic, and hormonal responses. We've got cortical sensory buffers that hold on to information about the currently present stimuli. We've got a working memory executive that keeps track of the short-term buffers, retrieves information from long-term memory, and interprets the contents of the short-term buffers in terms of activated long-term memories. We also have cortical arousal. And finally, we have bodily feedback – somatic and visceral information that returns to the brain during an act of emotional responding. When all these systems function together a conscious emotional experience is inevitable. (1987, p. 296)

Discussion on basic emotions is ongoing with Gadino (2006) providing ample ammunition against models proposed in various fields of study. In contrast, based on research literature and study of specific brain signals and universal nonverbal expression, Oatley and Johnson-Laird (1987) and Turner (2002) identify four basic emotions or innate emotions: happiness, fear, anger, and sadness. Combinations of these four basic emotions can lead to more complex emotions such as shame, jealousy, or pride. Turner and Stets (2006) support the existence of basic emotions and consider the possibility that more than four basic emotions might exist: "Yet, it is clear that there are primary or hard-wired [having a biological basis] emotions— at a minimum satisfaction-happiness, aversion-fear, assertion-anger, and disappointment-sadness (and perhaps others such as disgust, surprise, anticipation, excitement, and interest)" (p. 46). Humintell (2011) recognizes seven basic emotions "that have been scientifically proven to have a certain facial expression associated with [each one]" (p. 1). The seven basic emotions are anger, contempt, fear, disgust, happiness, sadness, and surprise (six of them, the exception being "contempt" appear in Ekman, 1999, "contempt" being then only considered as a candidate for basic emotions). Humintell offers "microexpression training" using an on-line program that prepares one to recognize emotions on others' faces as well as on one's own face.

While the controversy on the number of basic emotions continues, two facts are clear: 1) we are all emotional beings, and 2) a relationship exists between emotions, cognition, rationality, and feelings, regardless whether we regard them through impulse and/or consciousness of sociocultural norms (Sylwester, 1994). With respect to defining and expressing emotion in different cultures/societies, and "to join biology with cognitive science, development, and education so that education can be grounded more solidly in research on learning and teaching" (Fisher, Goswami, Geake, & Task Force on the Future of Educational Neuroscience, 2010, p. 68) I mention the monumental work of Fisher and his colleagues (Fisher et al., 2010; Fisher, Wang, Kennedy, & Cheng, 1998). Fisher et al. (1998) conclude that due to cultural variations in emotions and emotional development in humans in different parts of the world, one must take into consideration the collaboration between biology and cultural expression of emotions. I am impressed with the richness of the Chinese vocabulary to express emotions related to "shame," when contrasted with the vocabulary of native speakers of American English; some Mandarin words for describing "shame" have no parallel in English. I am also surprised by the Chinese treatment of "love" as primarily a negative emotion while the English-speaking treat love as a primarily positive emotion. Fisher et al. (1998) clarify that, despite unwillingness to "show off," individuals from Asian cultures have a positive and well-developed self-concept. In many ways, my Romanian background is very similar to the Asian perspective prohibiting self-promotion. Fisher et al. conclude that to be able to explain emotions and emotional development, we need to connect biology and culture.

Shifting attention to the newly developed field of educational neuroscience, Fisher et al. (2010) recommend establishing research teams involving experts from different areas such as biology, cognitive science, human development and education:

> Effective educational research requires that educators play a central role along with researchers in formulating questions and methods. Biology is central to this emerging field, informing educational practice in many ways through providing basic knowledge about body and brain as they relate to learning and teaching. (p. 77)

My hope is that with the development of new brain research techniques, such as the neuroimaging method called functional magnetic resonance imaging (fMRI—a type of specialized MRI scan used to measure the hemodynamic response—a change in blood flow), we will learn ways to 1) diminish the personal bias of the researcher while addressing cultural dimensions of the person being researched, and 2) determine trends in physiological responses leading to emotional investment in learning. Just imagine being able to "see" the emotional cascade prior to a student's decision to give up on a task and use scaffolding (Vygotsky, 1978), according to measurable need rather than just teacher's instinct/gut feeling.

Emotional Versus/and Rational Responses

So, where are the brain sites for emotional responses? ... for rational decisions? Are these the same sites? If the answer is no, are the sites for emotional response located in close relationship and/or connected to the site(s) controlling mental complex functions? What is the connection between thinking and feeling? I know that these functions point to the brain (the traditional statement within the biology majors society: "I love you from the bottom of my ... hypothalamus" or "my brain" (Society for Neuroscience, 2005 December), and that is more correct than relating love to the heart – sorry for the inconvenience to individuals celebrating valentines, poets, song writers and others, who keep the heart as their symbol for love. I am extremely curious about research development in this area as we further use fMRI scans (also see Dan Vergano's article in *USA Today*, 2006). These magnetic resonance scans use neuroimaging – the ability to visually display enhanced brain activity measured by enhanced blood flow following a certain stimulus (Wikipedia, 2011, February). National Geographic (2011) offers a look at the human brain, "a jelly-like mass of fat and protein weighing about three pounds (1.4 kilograms)" (p. 1), as seen from the outside and the inside, and correlates basic structures with functions. It seems that the frontal lobe is the center for reasoning and problem-solving, as well as the emotional center for love, once the signal is given from the activated hypothalamus. Scientists identify two brain areas – the amygdala and prefrontal cortex as playing key roles in the emotions associated with phobias (Society for Neuroscience, 2005 February). Genes to Cognition Online (2011) emphasizes the role of the amygdala in fear processing, emotion processing, learning, fight-or-flight response, and reward processing.

Materials for Teaching While Addressing Students' Emotions

BrainU housed in the Department of Neuroscience at the University of Minneapolis, an excellent public resource in the areas of cognition and emotion, uses effective contemporary pedagogy to teach about the brain. Geared toward teachers, BrainU offers professional development activities in addition to making materials and resources available via its web site.

BrainU (2011) with its *Teacher Guide: Mirroring Emotions* identifies two interlinked systems that respond to stimuli through emotions: the limbic system, which includes the amygdala - fast responding, and the prefrontal cortex which is in charge of stimuli that are processed for a longer time (also supported by research by De Martino, Kumaran, Seymour, & Dolan, 2006, on bias, context/frames, and rational decision-making in gambling situations). While the amygdala is responsible for the immediate, automatic emotional response,

...humans engage the rational observation and decision-making area of the cortex to choose the course of action that can best react to the full context of the emotional information. This does require additional synapses and hence time to be able to cognitively recognize an emotion. Hence, making the 'I feel sad' statement only comes after the introspective process of examining one's thoughts and feelings... (BrainU, 2011, p. 4).

The two systems (limbic and prefrontal cortex) seem to allow (or should I use "encourage") emotional bias and are intrinsically linked by parallel circuits. The limbic system seems to be responsible for regulating emotions and also is involved in basic learning (Oltmanns & Emery, 2003). In order to learn, i.e., make new memories by enhancing synapses, one has to have the coincidence of the event or knowledge activating synapses and an emotional valence/salience activating at least for a subset of the same synapses. We still cannot measure exactly which synapses are active with a specific piece of knowledge. De Martino et al. (2006) show a "significant correlation between decreased susceptibility to the framing effect [the manner in which options are presented] and enhanced activity in the orbital and medial prefrontal cortex" (p. 686). In other words, there is a relationship between lowering the effect of amygdala and enhancing the effect of rational decision-making with the help of prefrontal cortex.

I personally like the position of Frijda (2008) who counters the traditional approach to emotions and cognition as opposing faculties. Instead, Frijda sides with contemporary psychology that proposes "how intimately information processing and acting, reacting emotionally, and appraising emotional meanings, and goal setting and pursuing impulsive aims and desires are intertwined" (p. 81). We need to move away from the confusion showing correlation between emotion-cognition distinctions as unconscious-conscious information processing. I would add that in addition to the brain link between limbic system and prefrontal cortex, once we talk or think about emotions, we are actually discussing feelings, and as such they are already rationalized/processed through cognitive mechanisms. Accepting the interlinked system of emotion and cognition/rationality makes a lot of sense to me.

Pathways for Emotions

Most pathways are still under research, and others such as love (see Wikipedia 2011, March) are too complex to describe here for the biochemistry associated with attachment, lust, and attraction experienced during love.

Hence, I focus and describe two emotions with great significance to learning: pleasure (Wow! I've got it!) and pain (Oh, no! I have to take physics again after failing it twice!). Pleasure and pain are relatively simple emotions influencing students' involvement in learning in general, and learning science and mathematics, in particular. Both have biologically (i.e., physiologically) defined reflexive (or instinctive) behaviors, seemingly following a well-defined emotional pathway through the amygdala that is independent of sociocultural norms and rational thinking. I do not say that thinking cannot modify the emotional pathway, or that it should always be modified.

For readers who want to deepen their understanding of the different parts of the nervous system and their role in emotional expressions, I recommend Larsen, Berntson, Poehlmann, Ito, and Cacciopo (2008). Although Larsen et al. indicate that the exact pathways are not understood, negative emotions have been found to increase health problems, including enhanced susceptibility to infections. These authors ask researchers to move from researching the psychophysiology of emotions through autonomic, somatic, and central nervous system activity in isolation, to researching using a combined approach that blends with other systems such as the immune system (the need to understand the relationship between negative emotions and health problems). For a basic text on neurobiology of emotions, I recommend LeDoux (1987) as he uncovers three pathways for emotions: stimulus evaluation, bodily expression, and conscious experience through text and schematic drawings. His exploration takes an historical perspective that connects advances in different areas of biology, technology, and medicine.

Pleasure

In order to understand the relationship between our brain and pleasure, I expand on the subject of neurotransmitters – chemicals that are involved in the transmission of signals from one neuron to another, or from the ending of an axon to motor neurons to a muscle fiber. I focus on dopamine and endorphin, two related neurotransmitters (King, 2011), which are strongly connected to the feeling of pleasure.

Dopamine is a neurotransmitter that is produced in the brain – midbrain and brain stem, and much less in the medulla of adrenal glands. It is involved in many brain functions such as cognition, voluntary movement, motivation, punishment, and reward. The pathway of dopamine involves areas in the brain that include the limbic system and prefrontal cortex, and the amount of dopamine release is proportional to the difference between event expectation and actual perception. In other words, more dopamine is released in situations when our perception of an event exceeds expectations related to the event, and the dopamine signal adds to other activated circuits resulting in reinforcement or weakening of synapses accordingly. It is no wonder that we tend to learn behaviors that increase dopamine release and lead to rewards and pleasure/euphoria. Dopamine decrease in the frontal lobes results in diminished neurocognitive functions, such as a decline in memory, attention, and problem-solving, in the prefrontal cortex. This could be related, in specific situations and depending on many other circuits involved, with attention deficit disorder. For more information consider, Oltmanns and Emery (2003) and Wikipedia (March 8, 2011).

Also producing a sensation of pleasure is the work not only of endorphins (its name comes from its effect similar to morphine, as it is an endogenous-morphine), but also relatively short chains of amino acids or neuropeptides, synthesized by the pituitary gland and hypothalamus. Endorphins block nerve cells from releasing pain signals, and, as such, increase the feeling of pleasure. Exercise, excitement, pain, love, orgasm and consumption of spicy food release endorphins in humans (Wikipedia, March 15, 2011). Runners may perceive the runner's high (Prof. Janet Dubinsky, personal communication) because the release of endorphins suppresses the pain associated with muscle fatigue and potential tissue damage. On the web page of C. George Boeree (2009a) endorphin is portrayed as the neurotransmitter that "allows bears to hibernate." Heroin, an opioid that binds to endorphin's receptor sites, has the same effect as endorphin—it slows down heart rate, respiration, and metabolism, sometimes "all down to nothing," resulting in "permanent hibernation," or even death by overdose.

Consistent with the human tendency to look for positive emotions such as happiness, Daniel Gilbert (2007), Professor of Psychology at Harvard and director of the Social Cognition and Emotion Laboratory states: "We experience emotions, we all want to be happy all the time." He clarifies a need for balance "So, emotions are a kind of mental compass that points us in a certain direction. A compass that always pulls north would be useless, no? So emotions are not always stuck on 'unhappy'" (p. 61). Extrapolating the compass metaphor, I conceptualize mini compasses showing relationships between pleasure/happiness and pain, with a general compass summarizing data from all the mini-compasses into one general feeling. Gilbert focuses on north/south as the pleasure/pain scale; I extend the metaphor to include combinations of emotions resulting in east/west dimensions.

Pain

As we travel through life, we all try to avoid pain, a "universal experience" (Society of Neuroscience, 2008, p. 49) that relates a physiological and emotional response to unpleasant stimuli. Initially, a reflexive warning and withdrawal mechanism protects us from harmful stimuli (Fields, 2007), and our society is constantly developing medicine to reduce or neutralize physical and emotional pain. Pain has positive benefits as it helps us escape danger and avoid or shorten harmful encounters. For example, you sense that you have stubbed your toe on a rock before you feel the pain from it. With the release of hormones, pain causes increased heart rate and blood pressure. Specialized free nerve endings called nociceptors in the periphery are activated by painful mechanical, biological, chemical, thermal and electrical primary stimuli (Helms & Barone, 2008; Society for Neuroscience, 2008). Two different fiber systems carry the signals. The A fibers carry normal level sensory information on temperature, pressure, vibration, and touch. The C fibers carry the painful level stimuli. The A fibers exhibit a fast response, even before a person perceives the pain, while the C fibers have a slow response, producing constant pain (Figure 3.2).

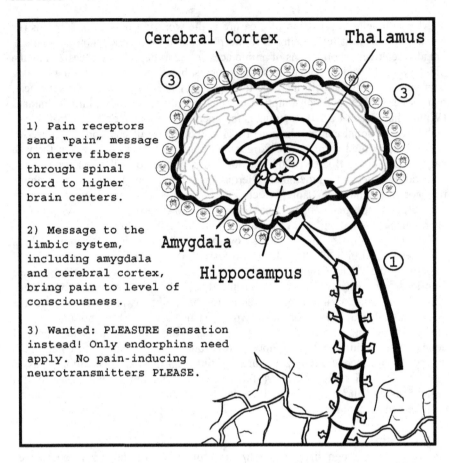

Figure 3.2. "Ouch" pathway with brain surrounded by Wong-Baker FACES pain rating scale.

Pain receptors are on the free nerve endings in skin, muscle and internal organs. The electrical signals from them are conveyed to the stated brain areas where they are perceived, i.e., interpreted by our brains as real world events impinging on our body (Hopley & van Schalkwyk, 2006). So pain receptors are on the 'far' end of the nerve fibers that carry the painful information to the spinal cord where it is relayed to higher brain centers. "The basic sensation of pain occurs at the thalamus level. It continues to the limbic system (emotional center) and cerebral cortex, where pain is perceived and interpreted" (Helms & Barone, 2008, p. 40). When activated (i.e., connecting to specific receptors in specific parts of the central nervous system), neurotransmitters such as glutamate, γ-aminobutryic acid, and tachykinins are known to induce pain. Drugs are continuing to be developed to neutralize receptors or create conditions in which the drugs would block the binding of neurotransmitter to the specific receptor, in order to diminish the feeling of pain. Within certain discrete central nervous system circuits, the human body has a natural chemical pathway to manage pain by releasing endogenous opioids such as endorphins. As chronic pain involves both affective and cognitive traits allowing increased susceptibility to a stimulus, due to a "build-up of the electrical response in the central nervous system" (p. 42), chronic pain is relatively poorly understood, and is difficult to assess, treat, and monitor.

Looking at what we know about emotional pain (and the affective side of neuroscience in general – e.g., see Dalgleish, 2004), we seem to need improved techniques to pinpoint emotional pathways in the brain as these relate to pain and learning. I believe science and mathematics educators could use the Wong-Baker FACES pain rating scale that allows individuals to relate emotional/cognitive pain resulting from interactions among physical, psychological, cognitive, and emotional networks to faces and numbers (Helms & Barone, 2008, p. 45) prior to instruction.

Emotional Intelligence and Emotional Literacy – Crossing Emotion/Rationality Distinction

As a very emotional person, I hoped for a supportive message about our knowledge regarding emotions from the literature on emotional intelligence. Goleman (1995) suggests using Peter Salovey's framework encompassing five main domains in order to define emotional intelligence: 1) knowing one's emotions; 2) managing emotions; 3) motivating oneself; 4) recognizing emotions in others; and 5) handling relationships (p. 43). Goleman's concern with individuals' lack of emotional literacy leads him to propose an easy-to-use, six-step recipe focusing on rationalizing one's response to a challenging stimulus - not allowing our emotions to rule our behavior through the direct loop when thinking is necessary. During the "red light" period, an emotionally literate individual is to "stop, calm down, and think before you act" (p. 276). The four-stage "yellow light" requires restating the problem, defining feelings, setting a positive goal, and finding multiple possible solutions, including consequences. Finally, during the "green light" period one recommends moving forward using the best plan. In the case of immediate physical danger, when a "fight-or-flight" response is necessary (from visual sensory center to amygdala to physical response such as increased heart rate and large muscles prepared for action - p. 19), Goleman emphasizes the hand-in-hand relationship between the emotional and the rational sides in *Homo sapiens*.

Is emotional intelligence identical to emotional literacy? It is quite hard to answer this question based on current literature. Goleman (1995) uses these terms interchangeably to mean human ability to manage emotions using a variety of techniques. In a later study, Salovey, B. Detweiler-Bedell, J. Detweiler-Bedell and Mayer (2008) acknowledge that because of the novelty of the domain of emotional intelligence, we experience definitions streaming from different areas of expertise with different lenses. These authors ask researchers to contribute to the development of a reliable measuring instrument because research in this area might shed some light on what it really means to be smart in the 21st century. Grewal and Salovey (2005) provide us with an elegant history of emotional intelligence and the different instruments developed to try and measure/quantify it. Even so, we do not have an instrument that is able of capturing the richness of human emotional intelligence ... yet. Matthews' research (2004, 2005) looks at the development of emotional literacy as a necessary step in communication between sexes during active science learning in co-education. Using large scale research with students ages 11-14 in England in active, student-centered science classrooms, Matthews concludes that promotion of emotional literacy has benefits in terms of students' understanding of classmates of opposite gender, students' enjoyment in collaborative work, and an increased tendency to offer academic support to peers, all leading to better science learning.

Winerman, (2006) adds research data from fMRI results that reveal that verbalizing feelings (lighting up the right ventral lateral prefrontal cortex) reduces emotional distress resulting from perceived social rejection (by suppressing anterior cingulate cortex that produces emotional pain). In other words, now we even have empirical evidence that supports the notion of using emotional intelligence/emotional literacy to support learning.

Learning Science and Mathematics: Balancing Emotions and Cognition
How are emotions, cognition, emotional intelligence and literacy folded into learning science and mathematics? Based on the literature mentioned previously we understand that there is a tight connection between the limbic system and cortex, or between emotions and rationality. We have also known for a long time that just possessing the ability to think critically and problem-solve does not necessarily translate into willingness to solve mathematics word problems or get involved in engaging in science inquiries. The affective domain seems to be as important as cognitive domain, meaning that students must "buy into" investing the energy in thinking critically and problem-solving.

Csikszentmihalyi (1990) develops the idea of flow for successful learning by looking at the dynamics between the perceived skill to perform a task (x axis) and perceived challenge of the task at hand (y axis) (Figure 3.3).

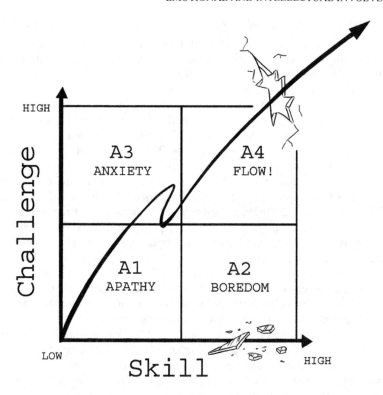

Figure 3.3. The four domains of Csikszentmihalyi (1990).

He examines the dynamics of positive and negative emotions resulting from the interplay of human perception of skill and challenge of task. Csikszentmihalyi defines the area of diagonal of these axes as the "flow channel" when a person perceives the experience as enjoyable (pleasure), however unstable. In the flow channel are two extreme possibilities – A_1 when challenge is low and perception of skill is also at a low level, and A_4 when both challenge and skill are perceived as high. The other possibilities are A_2 – boredom resulting from the perception of high skill and low challenge, and A_3 – anxiety resulting from perceptions of high challenge and low skill. Boredom and anxiety are not positive states, and when these emotions arise, individuals try to return to the flow channel, sometimes taking some unconventional pathways such as investing energy and creativity in becoming the class clown, solving problems in the text that are harder (the ideal student), or choosing another activity that does not connect with class tasks. Since we want students to learn at their highest-level possible when they perceive their skill as high, we should immerse them in challenging learning opportunities (Moscovici, 2003a). We should focus on the A_4 area. As humans face multiple tasks at any given point in their lives, we might need to look into the psychology of the dynamics of being engaged in multiple simultaneous tasks.

While Csikszentmihalyi (1990) focuses on feelings resulting from perceptions of skills and challenge of the task at hand, Heschl (2002) analyzes the survival of the most intelligent species on earth, *Homo sapiens,* over time. He addresses the dynamic nature of intelligence that today includes other skills (e.g., social abilities). We may have to redefine what is meant by "fittest" in Darwin's "survival of the fittest" concept, in the past usually understood in a physical sense to mean the "most intelligent." Darwin's "survival" as reproductive power is not necessarily an indicator in today's society in which educated or "intelligent" individuals are concerned with overpopulation. The definition of "fittest" may need to extend to include interpersonal communication.

I would like to remind the reader of the necessary skills required of the 21st century global high school graduate (The Partnership for the 21st Century Skills, 2006). The list of what it means to be equipped with the skills necessary to lead a successful and useful life might be a viable recipe in our century for "intelligence." In other words, a high school graduate who understands science and mathematics and the role of these subjects in every-day life is technologically literate and innovative/creative; possesses interpersonal skills, high morality and work ethics; and we should add, has emotional intelligence and literacy (Goleman, 1995; Matthews, 2004; 2005) is the kind of student we want to graduate and consider "fit" (according to Darwin) or "intelligent" (Heschl, 2002) for today's world.

Literature on the relationship between affective and cognitive domains on learning is extensive. In their chapter entitled, "We feel, therefore we learn: The relevance of affective and social neuroscience to education," Immordino-Yang and Damasio (2008) define "emotional thought" as "the platform for learning, memory, decision-making, and creativity, both in social and nonsocial contexts" (p. 193). Although I would challenge the "nonsocial" contextual aspect, due to my Vygotskyan perspective (Vygotsky, 1978) that defines even our inner thoughts as social because we use language that is socially defined, I agree with the concept of "emotional thought" interacting with rational thought on one side, and with body processes on another side, and as such influencing health-related processes.

Isen (2008) also discusses the relationship between positive affect and problem-solving, and suggests that higher levels of neurotransmitter dopamine associated with reward mechanisms might play "an important role in mediating many of the cognitive effects of positive affect that have been observed" (p. 568). Isen, however, underlines the point that we should not analyze these relationships in simplistic ways and we should take into consideration elements such as situational context as being able to follow existing established patterns to enhance positive affect.

Coming from the field of psychiatry and as an energy expert, Orloff (2005) analyzes sources of energy in our lives. She encourages us to maximize the flow of positive energy, and combat and reverse potentially negative energy emotions, such as fatigue, stress and fear, into positive energies such as vibrancy, strength and love. According to her, positive energy can be harnessed by "nurturing forces from within, such as compassion, courage, forgiveness and faith … or from without: supportive friends, creative work, the ability to laugh, or vibrant sexuality" (p. 5). I loved Orloff's chapter on ways to detect "energy vampires" or "leaches" and how to protect our positive energy from them. Breathing deeply, defining clear boundaries, staying neutral, distancing or deciding to walk away from a harmful situation, removing negative energy from our system, and exercising visualization are all good ways to avoid possible leaches looking to take advantage of our positive energy sources. In an interview, Vanzant, an ordained minister who is an author and inspirational speaker, also identifies love as "the most positive energy we have" (Orloff, p. 157). Vanzant also highlights the ability of humans to "generate positive energy" in themselves, energy that she calls qi – "an inner light that radiates through us, the noble essence of every being" (p. 156). Coming from poverty and being the child of a very ill single black woman in the 1950s, Vanzant learned to transform anger, fear, and disempowerment into positive energy by learning from experience and becoming wiser and more loving (similar to emotional intelligence/literacy loops in Golemen, 1995).

In learning science and mathematics (and in learning in general), we experience disequilibrium and the need to accommodate new information into our knowledge schema (Glasersfeld, 1988, 1989). As such, a learner experiences challenges while simultaneously assessing personal competency (Csikszentmihalyi, 1990). Anxiety/fear might result from a conditioned state in which a learner's evaluation of competence always falls short while the evaluation of the challenge is always at the high level (therefore installing the conditioned stage). This anxiety/fear leads to "acute mental stress" (LeDoux, 1987, p. 318 based on research reported by Brod, Fenel, Hejl, & Jirka, 1959 while studying complex mental arithmetic), which follows the process of "diffuse sympathetic activation" (part of the autonomic nervous system) resulting in increased heart rate, dilated pupils, and increased secretion of adrenalin and noradrenalin (among others).

Tobias (1987) examines the reaction of the sympathetic branch of the nervous system, in instances of a person's inability to think during the panic attack of the mathematics phobic student when faced with an impossible challenge:

The understanding and recall patterns have become cluttered with emotions. There is an inability to think, but not because the 'hardwire' is inadequate. The input, memory, and understanding and recall systems are just as good as they were before. But because the pathways have been blocked, you cannot remember (p. 7).

In a stage of high anxiety/panic attack, the sympathetic (autonomic) division of our nervous system reacts so as not to allow access to what one knows (lasting for about 20-30 minutes), and thus an individual without intervention is set up for failure and continuation of the conditioned pattern. Tobias suggests that we can use the brain to reverse this pattern by recognizing the emotional cascade involved in a panic attack, which impacts one's ability to problem-solve (self-monitoring), as well as engage in actual problem-solving, and to track associated emotions (thoughts and feelings). Specifically, Tobias recommends using a divided page in a notebook, writing on one side one's emotions and on the other side the cognitive domain. Then one can analyze relationships between thoughts and feelings, as well as flaws in the solving of the mathematics problem (giving yourself permission), and being able to anticipate difficulties and take steps (self-mastery).

Questions Set 3.3:

1. Can you relate a positive emotional state with learning science and/or mathematics? Describe the situation in two to three paragraphs.
2. Identify emotional and cognitive cascades from the recognition of an external stimulus(i) and relate these to brain mechanisms leading to the feeling of pleasure and to the concept of flow (Csikszentmihalyi, 1990).
3. Think about a negative emotional state resulting from your inability to solve a problem in mathematics or to master a concept in science.
4. Identify emotional and cognitive cascades from recognition of external stimulus and relate these to brain mechanisms leading to the feeling of pain/anxiety and to the concept of flow (Csikszentmihalyi, 1990).
5. Could you change the negative emotional state into a positive experience using ideas presented in this chapter (e.g., Mallow's desensitization and relearning, 1986; Goleman's steps for reaching emotional literacy, 1995; Orloff's recommendations to increase positive energy, 2005)? Describe in detail how you would do this.

EMOTIONAL AND COGNITIVE ENGAGEMENT DURING SCIENCE AND MATHEMATICS LEARNING

There is no doubt that *Homo sapiens* is an emotional and cognizing being, and that as such, we need to take into consideration both these dimensions when optimizing learning (Frijda, 2008). As learning is based on disequilibrium (Glasersfeld, 1988, following Piaget) and accommodation, we may encounter a potentially painful situation when facing a cognitive challenge. When people are faced with a similar situation, previous knowledge and experiences shape response through certain emotional pathways. An emotional cascade might be triggered by a word, such as, in my case, stoichiometry or "two trains leave cities A and B travelling toward one another..." and place the individual in conditioned phobia (Nevid et al., 2003; Oltmanns & Emery, 2003) or neurosis due to "persistent experiences of negative effect" (Boeree, 2009b). As an integral part of learning, one (a learner) should make an effort to identify negative emotional patterns related to learning certain subjects or sub-subjects and diminish or cancel the effect of phobia/neurosis that tends to freeze the cognitive part of brain from solving the problem at hand (LeDoux & Hirst, 1987; Tobias, 1987). Desensitization and relearning (Mallow, 1986), self-monitoring and self-mastery (Tobias, 1987), steps to emotional literacy or rationalizing emotions (Goleman, 1995; Matthews, 2005), and even learning how to transform potential negative emotions related to challenges into positive emotions related to learning (Csikszentmihalyi, 1990; Orloff, 2005) are some ways in which learners can overcome personal challenges and open themselves to learning science and mathematics.

In order to enhance learning of science and mathematics, we need to connect the learning process more to pleasure and satisfaction (Csikszentmihalyi, 1990), and less to pain, in other words to help the "mental compass" turn toward pleasure (Gilbert, 2007). Increased dopamine release as a reward system creates the pleasure/euphoria resulting from "I got it!" or "I solved the problem and got the correct result." The excitement following a learner's success leads to release of endorphins that increases the feeling of pleasure by blocking nerve cells to release pain signals (Boeree, 2009a). Multiple successful learning experiences in science and/or mathematics might create the conditioning needed, so that just mentioning the words science and/or mathematics might result in dopamine release and increased cognitive functions (Oltmanns & Emery, 2003). Though research of science attitudes and science learning show positive correlations (Rennie & Punch, 1991; Schibeci & Riley, 1986; Simpson & Oliver, 1990; Wilson, 1983), we need to look further into emotions and ensure equilibrated positive experiences for our students.

Repetitions of multiple unsuccessful experiences related to a science and or mathematics subject or sub-subject might result in the development of pain. By focusing on increasing pleasure resulting from learning science and mathematics, we reduce the possibility of unnecessary pain (there is a certain portion of pain resulting from discomfort during disequilibrium; however, this is a temporary stage).

In light of Csikszentmihalyi's (1990) idea of flow for successful learning, it is no wonder that research in the past has shown that having high expectations (high challenge) and building students' self esteem with respect to their ability to perform the task (high skill) lead to students increased performance in a specific area. We need to take Csikszentmihalyi's concept of flow (developed for a specific skill) and expand it to mirror human reality, meaning simultaneously solving multiple tasks involving variable perceptions of skill and challenge. Humans have priorities as to which task needs to be solved first, with specific tasks and challenges taking years, tens of years, and sometimes even lifetimes to solve (sometimes totally unsuccessful quests, such as in the case of scientists working all their lives to answer a question, and not being able to find any).

A last word – we need to work at changing the "norm" in the American population, which classifies individuals who work, study, and enjoy (have pleasure from) science and mathematics as abnormal. Just imagine a place where the norm is reversed, and individuals are expected to enjoy, study, get immersed in and plan to work in areas related to science and mathematics... I cannot think of any work area where science and mathematics do not play a key role, and being human is just science and mathematics at work. Thus, it seems to me that the missing ingredient is reinstating the pleasure one can extract form learning these subjects and focusing on the feelings of "intellectual pleasure and sense of accomplishment" (Minstrell, 2000, p. 472).

LEARNING TO TEACH/TEACHING TO LEARN SCIENCE AND MATHEMATICS

INTRODUCTION

This chapter develops the idea that learning to become a teacher of science and mathematics is a lifelong process. The science and mathematics teacher or educator who as an individual engages her students emotionally and intellectually in teaching the subject, involves herself in continuous learning in two main areas: 1) pedagogical content knowledge, PCK (Gess-Newsome & Lederman, 1999; Shulman, 1986), and 2) development of becoming a transformative intellectual (Aronowitz & Giroux, 1993; Giroux & Simon, 1989) practicing critical pedagogy (Freire, 1998; McLaren & Kincheloe, 2007). An educator needs to be continuously involved in action research (or in critical and documented self-inquiry) and in metacognition to learn these two areas. As with all learning, one needs to be open to challenges, disequilibrium, and the unpleasant feeling of reorganizing and modifying one's own existing knowledge web to accommodate new data.

This chapter also addresses the notion that the development of the seasoned science and mathematics educator requires addressing situations and building and rebuilding the teaching self over time during schooling as well as during beginning teacher support systems. This is in contrast with a process of creating the "microwaved" teacher, such as is happening with graduates from "alternative" or "fast-track" programs in California. These programs compete with traditional science and mathematics teacher preparation programs to attract credentialed candidates. Instead of competing to prepare the best beginning teachers, these programs tend to compete for getting more for less as well as for shortness of time and effort – for example offering a masters degree in teaching to individuals with no real teaching experience. Because of the competition to award more certificates/diplomas, the focus on the "alternative" programs has changed from learning and building a repertoire of instructional strategies that ensure successful survival in the first years of teaching, to completing coursework quickly (teaching license +/- masters degree).

DEFINING TEACHING AND LEARNING

A great friend of mine and a member of my doctoral committee, Dr. Nancy Davis from The Florida State University used cards in one of her courses to push her students, including me, to identify and define teacher versus learner roles. The cards that she used made us realize that the roles of teacher and learner were not well defined for situations such as a guide and a team member involved in learning from and with other teammates during a field trip. The symbolic way of using the journey (the trip) as the teaching and learning experience has remained with me all these years, and I have shifted the goal or purpose from finishing the journey or arriving at a pre-determined end point, to enjoying and learning during the journey.

The symbolic way of looking at teaching and learning situations as a journey of co-learners with various expertise areas clarified my requirements for being a teacher, a university professor, and a parent. I always have believed in my motto: "I cannot learn from you if you cannot learn from me." Individuals who have tried to teach me without knowing me or trying to follow my way of thinking and identifying gaps in *my* thinking could never succeed, resulting in negative energy accumulating on both sides (Moscovici, 2002a, 2002b). But, individuals who knew me and connected new subjects to what I knew, who could follow my geometry proof and question a stage that was incorrect, were successful in improving my knowledge web, and as such, in teaching me (Moscovici, 2002a).

I see teaching and learning as simultaneous processes taking place as individuals participate in a journey as respectful co-learners. Negative energy resulting from disequilibrium and emotional pain from the inability to "get it" immediately counteract positive energy and pleasure resulting from having a co-learner who scaffolds (Vygotsky, 1978) my personal journey and helps me reach intellectual pleasure (Minstrell, 2000). I see the end of a teaching career as the time when the teacher gets so involved in routines (assimilation – to use Piagetian term) that she does not let herself experience disequilibrium and the need for accommodation, getting into, hopefully, the A_4 flow point (high challenge, high perception of expertise - Csikszentmihalyi, 1990, see Figure 3.3), and learning.

TEACHING EVENTS– EARLY CHILDHOOD TIMES

I do not recall instances in which I was pretending to teach dolls or classmates as some of my friends would do by setting dolls in a semicircle or in rows and explaining things to them. Of course, the dolls remained quiet during my friends' presentations, none of them moving or trying to answer any of the rhetorical questions sprinkling my friends' monologues. When I was thinking about how it might be in school, (in my mind) dolls did not replace students, and knowing myself as a questioning individual, I could not imagine that the static representation of a class of dolls who obeyed all rules was realistic.

While I was not involved in teaching dolls, I remember instances in which I had issues with strict rules during my preschool years. My father worked until very late in the evenings, so I attended a preschool that allowed children to arrive around 7 am and stay until about 5:30 pm. I enjoyed the variety of games and being with my friends, however, I hated the "sleeping" time. I was not one to take naps during the day. I preferred playing outside or inside with available toys and games. Negotiations with preschool personnel led to an arrangement in which I had to lie down quietly on the mattress, however I did not have to sleep, in order to participate in the afternoon activities. This decision was better than the punishment that had followed my previous refusal to nap and disturbance of other children, in addition to keeping the preschool personnel very busy during naptime. I used my forced quiet time to plan afternoon games, rethink play techniques, imagine, and purposefully detach my brain from the napping situation (Figure 4.1).

Figure 4.1. "Lie down, stare at the ceiling and DO AS YOU'RE TOLD" time.

Preschool personnel's openness for negotiations offered me choices, and choices had consequences attached. It was no secret as to what might happen once I made my choices. I had to develop and use emotional literacy (Goleman, 1995) to make and act on the best choice.

Playing with other children helped me understand the role of tutoring, especially when the tutored child was part of my team. Giving pointers on how to improve practice proved to be an effective way to win games. I was also receptive to the pointers given to me by other children. Early on I learned that being tutored was not a sign of weakness, but a way to strengthen and build upon what I/we had – learning to become better. I also learned that tutoring was a two-way ticket as we shared our strengths with each other.

Questions Set 4.1:

1. Do you recall a similar situation before school age in which you were in the position to teach others or were taught in a way that was really geared toward using your strengths to improve other skills? Write one to two paragraphs.
2. In small groups discuss similarities and differences between shared experiences and write (as a group) one to two paragraphs summarizing these. Use graphics if necessary or helpful.
3. Create a table of experiences for the whole class and connect those to teaching science and/or mathematics.

LEARNING TO TEACH AND TEACHING TO LEARN SCIENCE AND MATHEMATICS DURING SCHOOLING YEARS

"Teacher for the Day" in Romania

A tradition in our elementary school (grades 1-8) in Romania was to ask for volunteers for the "teacher for the day" event, which occurred in late spring. The event name might be misinterpreted as none of the "volunteers" taught for a whole day. A volunteer taught only for about 30 minutes; the teacher and other "volunteer" students taught for the rest of the day. The reason for having "volunteer" teachers was to train troublemakers to be teachers and have them experience the teacher side of dealing with disruptive students. In other words, the teacher selected the "teacher for the day," and "volunteered" chosen ones to teach. Classmates were asked to behave "normally," including assuming the role of troublemaker even when their friend was the "volunteer" teacher.

In fourth or fifth grade I "volunteered" to teach mathematics, a subject in which I felt very comfortable. I studied the topic, solved the problems and thought I knew how to teach. Needless to say nothing went as planned. Students misbehaved in very obvious ways, many of them imitating what I was doing – asking infinite number of questions in order to clarify ideas, disregarding the needs of other students and not allowing the "teacher" (me, in this case) to finish her sentences. Students not offering responses looked puzzled by my questions. In addition, "she took my pencil," "he pushed me," and "she pulled my hair" continuously disrupted my attempts to continue what seemed to be a total catastrophe. I tried to use the board and list the names of the misbehaving students, however I gave up, as my list included almost all students in class.

There was no flow for teaching and learning (Csikszentmihalyi, 1990), and I soon realized that knowing the subject and being prepared in terms of content was just a small part of teaching. I needed expertise in pedagogy – something I did not know existed at that time.

Being Prepared at All Times and Parents' Roles

Since I can remember, I feared the grade book in Romania. With three names in alphabetical order on each page, once opened, multiple grades for the whole year could be entered. You might ask, why the fear…?

Teachers selected students to question orally about the topic of the day at the beginning of a class period. Some teachers just opened the grade book to a page and called on the three names on that page, indifferent to the fact that they might have questioned the same students the previous day. Other teachers skipped to a page looking for students who did not have oral grades. Selected students had no time to prepare their responses, and teachers in Romania had fantastic peripheral vision. They could see the student presenting the response near the blackboard AND, at the same time, students in class who gave hints to the presenters. As a student, the only way to cope with the probability of being selected was to try to be at least partially prepared at all times.

Once a grade for the oral examination was entered in the grade book, the students had to bring their personal grade book to the teacher daily for recording the grade. Parents had to sign their child's personal grade book daily, otherwise the teacher called the parents to find out the reason for the delay. Parents also had to sign near the grade of written tests and quizzes, acknowledging that they had received the information. The assumption for this practice was that parents worked with their children, and the teacher's notations would help them to improve their children's knowledge of the subject.

Mathematics Preparation for Entry Examination into High School in Romania

Following eighth grade, and in order to be accepted into high school in Romania, students took five examinations: written and oral examinations in Romanian, written and oral examinations in mathematics, and an oral examination in the history of Romania (today one can choose geography instead of the history of Romania). Students selected a small number of high schools to which they would apply. Average scores on the five examinations influenced acceptance into the highly sought schools. Small committees of high school teachers conducted the oral examinations, while the Ministry of Education (national testing) separately evaluated the written examinations.

I knew that acceptance into the high school of my choice (theoretical "college" Caragiale) required a minimum of 9.8 GPA (out of 10) on the high school entry examinations. My parents hired a mathematics tutor who was an expert in high school examination preparation for a few sessions to help me. He expected that I would review the mathematics required for the examination and define the topics in which I needed help, as he did not have time "to waste." Studying with friends and co-tutoring helped me refresh my memory on the majority of the mathematics examination topics.

The tutor, an elderly gentleman with a wealth of examination preparation experience, used an interesting approach. He asked me to solve the type of problem on which I was having trouble. While I was solving the problem, I was to "talk aloud" every step as I wrote my process, using mathematical language. Small scaffolds on his part, accompanied by wise questioning led me to the expected answer. The tutor did not "show" me how to solve problems and expect me to copy his technique, but helped me with my technique and my way of understanding and solving problems. While explaining his techniques (procedural knowledge) and the advantages of using them to shorten the problem-solving time, he emphasized the fact that I could always use my technique if I chose to, as it also led to the correct answer. When he had me calculate lateral areas and volumes of bodies resulting from rotations of two-dimensional geometric figures around specific axes, the mathematics tutor taught me analytic geometry, which was not needed for the entry examination. In the beginning we were cutting paper figures into certain shapes and rotating them (concrete). After a little time I felt comfortable using my imagination to perform these tasks (abstract). I took a special liking to analytical geometry and the need for precision in building and calculating areas and volumes of three-dimensional bodies. Knowing more than was required also helped me with my self-confidence.

I was successful with my entry examinations and entered the high school of my first choice: theoretical "college," Ion Luca Caragiale.

Chemistry Teaching for the Chemistry Special Class in High School

Once accepted into the theoretical "college" Ion Luca Caragiale, I began ninth grade in single-gender classes. The intent was that hot-blooded teenagers focus on their studies rather than being preoccupied with their image in the eyes of the other gender. Teachers strongly challenged us to stretch beyond our potential as they shifted from concrete examples, to patterns, to exceptions, applications, and so on. Based on our GPA in ninth grade, we chose an option of either realistic or humanistic emphasis. Within the realistic emphasis we had the option of enhanced mathematics (students thinking about engineering) or enhanced chemistry (students thinking about medicine or chemistry). I chose enhanced chemistry and was one of the students accepted to study in this emphasis. As part of our studies, we were required to submit and solve problems from the "Olympiad" journals for both mathematics and chemistry.

My chemistry teacher was an excellent pedagogue: for example, she began the lesson on electrolysis with a simple demonstration or laboratory, conducted with a student assistant. Provided with a solution of cupric chloride ($CuCl_2$), two carbon electrodes, and a battery, a little later we all smelled the "swimming pool" aroma near one of the electrodes and saw the red powdery smear on the other electrode. "What happens here?" was her opening question. As an enhanced chemistry class, we were allowed to redo experiments as well as change concentrations, as long as we discussed and got approval from the chemistry teacher. Discussion among us and with the teacher, who was not volunteering answers, led to the possibility of obtaining copper metal (Cu) and chlorine gas (Cl_2). Here are some examples of questions asked by the teacher while leading our learning of the concepts of anode, cathode, reduction, oxidation, and electrolysis, and while writing and balancing chemical equations on this reaction:

1) Wait a minute! You want to tell me that we begin with ions and end up with atoms? How do you explain that?
2) Are you telling me that every time you will have copper moving toward the same electrode? Why would that be? Are you sure?
3) What would happen if we switch the carbon electrodes? Are you sure? Does anyone thinks differently? Why would you think that?
4) How would the electrons move once the chloride ions arrived at the anode? How do chloride ions (Cl^-) get oxidized to Cl_2?

The teacher seemed to show the most pleasure when we students argued with each other. Then she would use the same questioning strategies to make us think and solve the puzzle.

Thinking about the honors chemistry classes attended by my sons many decades later, I concluded that none of them looked like my high school experience. Their teachers would come to class, present a long lecture on a subject, which was rarely followed by a confirming laboratory in which students knew the "correct results" before performing the prescribed experiment. The teacher was not interested in students' experiences, and any attempt to slow down the pace was not welcome, as they "had to cover lots of material." Summarizing his high school experience, my oldest son, Danny, wrote a note on his bedroom door stating, "At school, I listen to people I don't like, talking about things I do not understand."

Questions Set 4.2:

1. Can you recall a formal situation in which the teacher opened a science and/or mathematics subject by describing a problem and asking students to solve it as individuals or in small groups? Write one to two paragraphs describing the experience, including personal emotions, classroom climate, and teacher's attitude.
2. How did the teacher make use of students' different ways of solving the problem and how did she connect students' problem solving strategies to other possibilities described in the text? Write one to two paragraphs.
3. Identify questioning strategies used by the teacher who wants to find and comprehend students' ways to solve problems (uncover previous knowledge) and then builds on these to expand and/or introduce other ways.
4. After discussing in small groups, create a table of questioning strategies that can be used by science and mathematics teachers to uncover students' previous knowledge and use this to expand ideas or introduce new ones. Using Bloom's taxonomy, identify the cognitive levels of these questions.

TEACHER-CENTERED VERSUS STUDENT-CENTERED PEDAGOGY FOR SCIENCE AND MATHEMATICS

The publication of the *National Science Education Standards* (NSES) (NRC, 1996), a result of numerous deliberations among scientists, science education researchers, and science teachers, provided the science education community in the USA with the necessary support for using scientific inquiry in science classrooms: "Inquiry into authentic questions generated from student experiences is the central strategy for teaching science" (p. 31). This document emphasizes the collaborative aspect of an inquiry-based science classroom in which teacher and students co-investigate a question asked. It also defines the role of the students as the decision-makers at all stages of inquiry, from formulating a research question to data collection and interpretation, to presentation:

> Students formulate questions and devise ways to answer them, they collect data and decide how to represent it, they organize data to generate knowledge, and they test the reliability of the knowledge they have generated. As they proceed, students explain and justify their work to themselves and to one another, learn to cope with problems such as the limitations of equipment, and react to challenges posed by the teacher and by classmates. Students assess the efficacy of their efforts – they evaluate the data they have collected, re-examining or collecting more if necessary, and making statements about the generalizability of their findings. They plan and make presentations to the rest of the class about their work and accept and react to the constructive criticism of others. (NRC, 1996, p. 33)

What is the role of the teacher when students are engaged in these activities? NRC (1996) in the NSES indicates the role of the teacher as: "at all stages of inquiry, teachers guide, focus, challenge, and encourage student learning" (p. 33). As skilled observers of students, teachers facilitate and monitor student learning, and provide scaffolding according to student needs.

NSES also promotes a shift from students working alone to students working in groups with cooperation and collaboration, and from the teacher presenting material and findings to the teacher guiding and preparing students to develop and present findings. In summary, a change from students who are passive to students who are actively engaged in evaluating, expanding, and defending knowledge that they have developed; a change from teacher-centered to student-centered classrooms. Jackson (2009) points out that in most cases teachers do students' work, and because of that, they work harder than their students. Unfortunately, these teachers also deny students the opportunity to learn.

As teachers in the USA were unfamiliar with how this scientific inquiry could manifest in the classroom, the NRC (2000) published another document with classroom examples. Students could be guided through scientific inquiries in classrooms, paralleling the processes of research scientists in the field. At the classroom level a teacher needs to consider content standards, limited outside resources, students' limited knowledge on a specific subject, students' limited interest in the subject, and time allocation. The NRC defines five essential features of inquiry (p. 29), and expresses variations of the starting inquiry point in terms of learner self-direction to direction from teacher or material. These are the features of the science learner: 1) engaging in scientifically-oriented questions; 2) giving priority to evidence in response to questions; 3) formulating explanations from evidence; 4) connecting explanations to scientific knowledge; and 5) communicating and justifying explanations.

Principles and Standards for School Mathematics (NRC, 2000), also similar in its content and process, focuses simultaneously on mathematics content standards (e.g., numbers and operations, algebra) and process standards (problem-solving, reasoning and proof, communication). NRC defines six principles: 1) promoting equity, 2) developing a coherent curriculum, 3) using a variety of teaching techniques, 4) facilitating students' learning conceptually, factually, and procedurally, 5) using a variety of assessment strategies, and 6) employing appropriate and supportive technologies.

Two major research-based documents edited by Donovan and Bransford (2005a, 2005b) for science and mathematics, support the idea of science and mathematics teaching being focused on students' previous knowledge, support for students' development of conceptual frameworks and of procedural and factual knowledge, and students' use of metacognition for self-regulation and self-learning. Both documents support problem-based teaching, with students actively involved in learning and with the teacher facilitating this process. In other words, both documents promote having a student-centered environment with the teacher providing guidance and challenge when necessary.

LEARNING TO TEACH AND TEACHING TO LEARN SCIENCE AND MATHEMATICS: TEACHER PREPARATION PROGRAMS AND THE CLASSROOM

Teacher Preparation in Romania and Israel

In Romania, teachers emphasized science content. Prospective science and mathematics teachers at all levels had to show evidence of successful careers as students, and completion of their science and mathematics degrees with high GPAs. "Middle school" teachers needed to have at least a bachelor's degree in the subject; teachers at the high school level needed a master's degree in their subject. Individuals who wanted to teach studied education courses (e.g., psychology, sociology, pedagogy, assessment) or a "pedagogical module" after completing subject content studies. Teachers were required to complete this "module" within five years after beginning to teach. A teacher could reach Level 1 teaching (the highest) through testing on content courses, accumulation of years of teaching experience, and/or participation in professional development situations. Teachers tended to try to reach Level 1 as it ensured them a teaching position in the country, as the population was decreasing due to a relatively low birth rate and the tendency of young adults to seek employment in other European countries.

In Israel, two routes exist for science and mathematics teacher preparation: one for the individual interested in teaching in elementary and middle school, the other for individuals interested in teaching in middle and high school. Colleges (not universities) offer such courses and programs. Individuals, who want to become elementary school teachers in self-contained, lower grade classes, complete content courses in different areas as well as the methods courses. The elementary/middle school license requires completion of a content requirement (specific courses and a certain number of semester credits) for those wanting to focus on specific content such as science and/or mathematics. The practicum component is composed of two parts: observation/participation in the first semester followed by teaching (being the teacher of record for half days) for another semester. During the second semester, pre-service teachers (or teachers in training) are fully in charge of all the needs of their classes, including holding parent conferences, taking part in school activities, and determining final grades. An assigned mentor teacher helps them when they have questions, and weekly seminars ensure help from the support group and a seminar leader.

The secondary teaching route requires a bachelor's degree in the subject of the middle and high school level teaching, followed by two years (at half-time) of university level education and teaching methods courses. Science and mathematics content courses are totally separate from education/pedagogy courses, and are held on different campuses with differing cultures. A teacher holding a credential for secondary teaching can add another secondary teaching credential by successful completion of: 1) content courses determined by the Ministry of Education (e.g., in my case for secondary mathematics credential included Linear Algebra, Number Theory, and Euclidian/Non-Euclidian Geometry), 2) a methods course in the subject, and 3) an external evaluation conducted by a representative of the Ministry of Education for the specific subject.

In my case, a zoology professor from the Hebrew University of Jerusalem and a science educator with biology background who was teaching the methods course (Professor Pinhas Tamir, known as Pini) provided the only connections between content and pedagogy during my secondary biology and general science credential studies. The zoology professor conducted a one-semester teaching seminar using his experience as a teacher at the university level. The one-semester teaching seminar course focused on content correctness and teacher preparedness. The methods course focused on meeting student needs and continuously assessing student learning through the use of a wide range of questioning strategies. Pini [we use first names in Israel] used closed circuit TV to record and show us our teaching of two different small groups of students who were brought to the university for us: one group were students at a high achieving high school located on the Hebrew University campus and the other group were students at a vocational program in which students worked during the day and took evening courses to finish high school. My lesson focused on the effect of pathogens on crops. While teaching, I realized that what I had prepared was inadequate for the full time, high achieving students and excessively long for vocational school students. My teaching videos showed that I did not really listen to students' questions and did not develop the peripheral vision needed for teaching, and that being prepared for a "general" class did not prepare me to teach the specific students before me [my emotions ran high because of the teaching, and the videotaping]. "Focus on the students, Hedy, know what they know and build from that, read their faces, listen to them, and be open to their suggestions," said Pini. I did not know then that Pini actually had positioned me on a track to becoming a transformative intellectual (Aronowitz & Giroux, 1993; Giroux & Simon, 1989) who considers both students' challenges regarding content (intellectual stage) as well as challenges regarding social classroom norms (transformative intellectual stage).

Teacher Preparation in the USA

When I began my doctoral studies in science education (at Florida State University in 1991) with a focus on pre-service elementary school teacher preparation in science, I began researching college science classes for non-majors in science. Despite then-current knowledge about teaching and learning, actual teaching of college science and mathematics courses remained unchanged from historical traditions for course instruction. A three-credit course would meet three times a week for 50 minutes lectures or twice a week for lectures that lasted 75 minutes each time. Pam (one of my case studies in my dissertation) described her image of a non-major science class at a research university as a "large college lecture halls led by stiff uncaring instructors ready to deliver the material and then hurry off to their own research" (Moscovici, 1994, p. 163) (Figure 4.2).

Tobias and Tomizuka (1992) explain the logic behind the impersonal presentations of science (long lectures) happening at the university (college) level, which do not reflect the nature of historical discoveries, such as the case of the four fundamental laws of thermodynamics, concepts of gene and chromosome in genetics, or the concept of atomic number in chemistry and physics. Tobias (1990) also suggests that as long as we continue to present science and mathematics topics in this impersonal way, disconnected from students' experiences, we will continue having bright individuals avoid science and mathematics-related careers. Herreid (2001), a supporter of problem-based (case study) science teaching and learning at the university level, shares the memory of a discussion with a colleague. The colleague remembers his undergraduate days with the long lectures and memorization of facts as hurtful (P. 87). Herreid states, "it has never struck me until this point that the undergraduate experience with its lectures and labs where you are told what to do and what to learn was – there is no other way to say it – crippling" (p. 88). Commenting on what the current teaching method at the university produces, Herreid clarifies (2001):

A cadre of students who if they remember anything about science, it is facts, facts, and more facts that can be used to answer questions on "Jeopardy," "The Wheel of Fortune," and "Who Wants to be a Millionaire?" We produce people who can't see the reason why they need to understand mitosis or the Second Law of Thermodynamics because they know deep in their heads they will never need to know this. What good is this information? We clearly fail to convince them. It's not that they try to forget this information; it just never gets in their long-term memory banks. The lecture method just isn't up to the job. (p. 88)

A LECTURE HALL'S NEWLY ADOPTED
"NOSEBLEED" SECTION.

Figure 4.2. Impersonal presentations negating the journey of the discoveries part of scientific knowledge.

Reflecting on my college science courses at the university level in Israel, I remember mixed experiences. There were many "content experts" who thought that their role was to monologue the updated content to class. Teachers considered students' questions as "disruptions" and ignored them as much as possible. I also had professors who really wanted us to learn and question, such as the professor who taught the Animal Behavior courses and only used verbal testing. I recall the two Ben-Sasson professors, who were brothers, one teaching the biochemistry course (connected to immunology) and the other teaching the course on cancer. While the first one was famous for his research, he was a relatively "poor" teacher and he recognized this fact. "If you want a good teacher you get a course with my brother," he said. And he was correct – the cancer course was one of the highlights of my biology education, His brother, a professor who engaged us in our own learning, guided us in discussing the main concepts, supplied scaffolds as needed, using articles and texts (pre-Internet era!!!), and let us explore lines of thought in cancer research. Needless to say I respected both Ben-Sasson brothers for their abilities to identify and use their talents to promote biology education.

Why are we surprised that individuals who have never had a course in pedagogy, in most cases tend to do (teach) what was done (taught) to them? At the university level, there is no requierment for courses in teaching in order to teach. A PhD in a subject area (e.g., science discipline or mathematics) is deemed sufficient for an individual to "teach" the science or mathematics, respectively in the case of this example. There is also a difference in perspectives as to the role of the science professor. From a science content professor perspective (similar to the zoology professor who taught the teaching seminar during my secondary teacher preparation in Israel and Dr. Strauss in the USA in my dissertation – see Moscovici, 1994), the role of the science professor is to provide the most updated and correct content; students are responsible for learning and demonstrating their assimilation of the content. From a science educator's perspective, however, the role of the science professor does not end with correct and updated content—it continues with the professor providing the best situations for the students to learn the content, relate the content to their lives and use the learned content in new situations.

My First Year Teaching Biology in Israel

I really learned how to teach after finishing my methods courses and experiences as a teacher intern, and became a teacher with my own classroom. Just when I was hired to teach biology and mathematics in Jerusalem, the education minister of Israel decided to discontinue the biology textbooks, as none of the textbooks were successful in students' construction of understanding of dynamically developing biological knowledge. Teachers worked all summer that year to collect and organize articles appropriate for high school students with respect to content and reading levels. Long debates and disagreements among us led to a school year beginning without a whole set of articles. I was teaching two sections of regular biology, one section of special biology (a different curriculum for students with severe behavioral problems) and two sections of combined algebra and geometry.

In the regular biology class, I was having the time of my life. I thought that the articles were very good. After discussing Francesco Redi's experiments disproving spontaneous generation in 1668, I moved to an article about the elegant experiments conducted by Louis Pasteur with Claude Bernard in 1862 that led to "pasteurization" and provided proof for the germ theory. After (according to me) a very successful lesson in which I described the lines of thought in the article and engaged myself immensely, one of my best students approached me and said: "Hedy [in Israel we use first names], we don't have a clue what you are talking about! All these articles might be interesting, but they are about hard concepts that we cannot grasp—from the readings, or from your presentations. You seem to care about us learning the material, as well as care for the subject, and that is why I came to tell you that you are the only one who gets it."

Three months into the semester, I was a total failure as a teacher. What I found disturbing was the contrast between the pleasure and excitement I felt as a teacher talking about historical events that shaped modern biology, and the pain of seeing the students' lack of ability to comprehend these advances. We shared many instances of solidarity and laughter/joking together, instances that had the potential to release the high anxiety level during science learning (Brigido et al., 2010; Ritchie, Tobin, Hudson, Roth, & Mergard, 2011; Roth, Ritchie, Hudson, & Mergard, 2011), however the students were not able to learn the biological concepts that excited me so much. I had forgotten all that Pini taught me and became a slave to my own pleasure, showing, presenting and explaining, rather than helping my students to explore ideas. Teaching awards us the pleasure of involving students in learning, challenging and scaffolding their journey, while, at the same time feeling the pain associated with not being allowed to use the "let me tell you what I know" monologue, even if it is on the tip of our tongue. That is when my motto of "the more you do, the less they do, the less, they learn" began to form in my head. A correlate, "the more you do, the more you learn" explains why Joubert (1842) arrived to the conclusion that "to teach is to learn twice."

My Second Year Teaching in Israel: Low Level Algebra to the Uninterested

I was in my second year of teaching, learning exponentially every day. In one of my mathematics sections my students had behavioral problems or learning disabilities. "It does not matter what you teach them as nothing will come out of them," I was told by the chair of the mathematics department before the school year started. "Prepare, but do not be disappointed if the results do not measure with your efforts as students in this class either cannot understand algebraic/geometry concepts, or they just don't want to learn." As I began to know the students in this class and learned about their home conditions, aspirations and hobbies, I realized that there were some students who were very nice and quiet but had cognitive barriers, and there were students with potential who did not have the basic algebra concepts. These students had been taught procedures connected to algebraic thinking without the conceptual understanding underpinning the procedures. I decided to help the students, asking them to participate in a competition that would show the school that they could learn algebra and score no less than many of the lowest students in the "regular" classes on the testing done by the Ministry of Education in a few weeks. All students agreed to participate in the challenge.

These students' lack of understanding of basic algebraic concepts brought back memories – Ms. Bayer's concrete exercises that really helped me to understand the meaning of fractions. The next day I came to the algebra class with fruit – two oranges, three apples, and three bananas. I placed them on my desk and asked the students to develop expressions for them. Their eyes popped out; they looked at each other with big question marks on their faces, and raised their shoulders to say, "I don't have a clue." I understood it was too much, and decided to use the three bananas only. "What do you see?," I asked. "Bananas," answered the class. "A certain quantity?," I pushed further. "Yes, three," answered the class. "Three what?," I asked. "Three bananas!" answered the class. "How do you think I should write that? Can someone help me?," I continued. Immediately a student came and wrote on the board: "3 bananas." "Anyone disagree?," I asked. No hands went up. "Are you sure?," I asked using my skeptical tone. All students nodded "yes" and said "yes." "You are good!," I exclaimed as I took three apples out of my bag and placed them on my desk. "What do you see now? Do the three bananas represent what you see now?," I asked. "No, you added three apples," answered the class. "Hmm… How do I write it now? Does anyone have an idea?," I asked. Lots of volunteering hands were raised. Students were eager to participate, eager to answer. The lesson continued with much more positive energy, humor, questions and answers, until we had an algebraic expression on the board representing the fruits I had brought in the bag. Due to my personal laziness to write whole words such as "bananas," I had students write letters such as "b" for bananas, "a" for apples, etc. Students even designed an algebraic equation expressing the total number of fruits on my desk using y (total number of fruits) = 3b + 3a + … by counting the number of fruits, students replaced the unknown, y. In groups, they were able to write expressions and equations. Other groups found other available objects fitting the equations/expressions that the students wrote. Needless to say that I did not have to bring fruits for future lessons, however I used the smells and images that they held in their memories for the whole unit. Students' testing results allowed a small number of these students to choose the regular classes. What a prize!

If we only taught conceptually first… Thank you, Ms. Bayer for an excellent teaching example – I will always remember the relationship between a loaf of bread and fractions.

During that lesson with concrete objects (the fruit), I was in the flow of teaching and students were in the flow of learning (Csikszentmihalyi, 1990). As the teacher, I saw the challenge as high, and I knew I had the skill to do it (A_4 on Figure 3.3). Of course, my confidence for facing this challenge was based on students' willingness to show that they could master simple concepts in algebra (also in A_4). Having a sense of humor, developing a common goal, balancing challenge and ability, and inducing a sense of solidarity were evident during this algebra "fast track" preparation.

Looking at a recent body of literature in a study of a first year teacher's use of emotional rituals to create learning conditions, the work of Ritchie et al. (2011) and Roth et al. (2011) in the area of science education are essential.

Education as a Business in USA and Globally

A tendency in the USA (and globally) exists to treat education as a business. Many undergraduate courses have become packaged and delivered "on-line," the clear advantages being high enrollment of students (with more dollars coming to the university) and access (convenience to "take the course" from anywhere in the world and at any time). Unfortunately, no research is available that addresses the quality of these experiences in terms of student learning. My experience with students aged 18-22 has shown that they tend to exchange places to pass tests for their friends, work in groups and use all the materials available to answer on-line test questions. They have even been known to change the author name on a paper submitted a few semesters ago, and submit it as their own and earn full credit. In addition, many introductory non-major science classes are taught using large, impersonal lecture situations and an enrollment of hundreds to even over a thousand students (Moscovici, 1994). Teaching assistants are in charge of laboratory/exercise sections (for science) or exercise sections (for mathematics) in order to help students remember terminology and definitions, and/or formulae and their uses.

I believe that we have jumped into large lecture classes and fashionable on-line education before ensuring that the quality of education remains unchanged. According to my peers, teaching large classes face-to-face or "on-line" cannot address students' responses because of time issues. In both instances faculty tend to rely on multiple-choice testing to avoid the load of reading responses to essay questions. Science and mathematics are considerably more than long lists of vocabulary words, their definitions, and formulae to be remembered for a test. Multiple-choice testing has not advanced to the level of checking for higher order thinking skills, despite efforts in this area (Yeh, 2001), perhaps because initial attempts questioning such design, showed that to build this type of question one needs to provide the test taker with ample descriptive information and the four or five optional answers need to include possible misconceptions held by students. In other words tests need to be prepared by experts not only in the subject matter but also in teaching the subject.

When I think about checking for students' understanding, I think about the work of Wiggins and McTighe (1998) and their six facets to demonstrate understanding: the student 1) can explain; 2) can interpret; 3) can apply; 4) has perspective; 5) can empathize; and 6) has self-knowledge (p. 44). Tests that check for these six aspects of understanding are something that we can only look forward to seeing in the future.

In addition to the problem of impersonal content presentations for which students' learning is not the main focus, there is also the problem of university professors remembering how they built conceptual understanding of their subject and a tendency to focus primarily on procedures. In science, university professors begin with a formula – an abstract concept that encompasses relationships among variables that were named and explored before the "birth" of the formula. In mathematics, university professors (and because of them, elementary school teachers) begin with procedural rules (also emphasized in U.S. mathematics textbooks) that can help us speed-solve a problem once we understand it. Ma (1999) in mathematics and Minstrell and van Zee (2000) in science conclude that the teaching of science and mathematics typically does not consider the students' background knowledge, does not involve the students in problem-solving/inquiries, does not involve the social aspect of learning (having students discuss and argue various solutions), and does not promote students' understanding of others' learning or build self-knowledge via metacognition. Ma (1999) and van de Walle (2004) suggest that teaching mathematics conceptually would change the way mathematics learning takes place in the elementary school classroom. Ma (2001) underlines the fact that when one teaches arithmetic, one begins with an abstract mathematical expression, called "problems" in U.S. jargon—(see Carroll and Murray, 2011, slide #10, in which expressions/exercises such as 192 - 40 are called "problems"), instead of a problem that has a concrete side in the story that relates to students' lives. The student is being denied the opportunity to translate a word problem into a mathematical expression (or perform "lie shi"). Ma is concerned that arithmetic is disappearing in the USA, while in other countries such as China (Ma's experience) and Romania (my personal experience) arithmetic is taught— the concept is taught first and the procedure follows with the use of arithmetic word problems. As there are lots of procedural ways to speed up solving mathematical expressions, students should think and choose for themselves what makes more sense to them. In my case, I can say that Ms. Bayer, my elementary school teacher succeeded in facilitating my conceptual understanding and instilled a love for arithmetic. She taught me to think.

Shortage of Mathematics and Science Teachers in the US

In the USA, the shortage of science and mathematics teachers presents us with a need to prepare science and mathematics teachers faster than traditional programs are able to do. When I arrived at the California State University – Dominguez Hills in 1999 (before the "No Child Left Behind" [NCLB] act), we had emergency permit teachers who were required to finish content and pedagogy requirements for teachers credentialing within five years. Some teachers finished in less than five years; others took longer. While they were enrolled in credential courses, emergency permit teachers had the opportunity to try what they were learning in the methods course in their own classrooms. They received feedback from the professors at the same time as they were teaching. Some emergency permit teachers withdrew from teaching, as they felt extremely unprepared to teach misbehaving urban students without any teaching experience, mentoring, or support from their school's administration. With NCLB legislation (U.S. 107th Congress, 2002), emergency permits disappeared and all teaching credential candidates had to have proof of content knowledge prior to being accepted in a credentialing program and being hired for a teaching position as a teaching intern. Teaching credential programs began competing for candidates by shortening their programs and providing the most goodies (e.g., a teaching credential and master's degree in teaching). "Alternative" programs, supported by grant money, popped up everywhere, again, all offering a long list of goodies such as stipends, money for books, a combined credential and master's in teaching, and shorter program length, "Microwaving" teachers without considering teacher needs and lack of maturity regarding classroom management, and other necessary experiences for becoming good beginning teachers, became the focus.

POWER RELATIONSHIPS AND CRITICAL PEDAGOGY INVOLVED IN
TEACHING SCIENCE AND MATHEMATICS

The foundation for my thinking rests with Yukl (1989) and Foucault (1979, 1980) with respect to the area of power relationships; and Grundy (1987), Freire (1990, 1998), and Giroux and his colleagues (Aronowitz & Giroux, 1993; Giroux & Simon, 1989) in the area of critical pedagogy.

Two major ideas in the area of power relationships left significant imprints on my perspective when analyzing science and mathematics teaching situations: Yukl's definition of power relationship, and Foucault's statement that power and knowledge are interrelated and relational. The powerful influence of these men's ideas on my thinking leads me to feature them in this book.

Yukl (1989) defines the power relationship as:

...an agent's potential influence over the attitudes and behavior of one or more designated target persons. The focus of the definition is on influence over people, but control over things will be treated as one source of power. The agent is usually an individual, but occasionally it will be an organizational subunit. (p. 14)

Foucault (1979) provides insight on the interdependence between knowledge and power, and the inevitable fact that power dynamics exist in any relationship, whether we want them or not:

Perhaps too, we should abandon a whole tradition that allows us to imagine that knowledge can exist only where the power relations are suspended and that knowledge can develop only outside of its injunctions, its demands and its interests. Perhaps we should abandon the belief that power makes mad and that, by the same token, the renunciation of power is one of the conditions of knowledge. We should admit rather that power produces knowledge (and not simply encouraging it because it serves power or by applying it because it is useful); that power and knowledge directly imply one another; that there is no power relations without the correlative constitution of a field of knowledge, nor any knowledge that does not presuppose and constitute at the same time power relations. (p. 27)

Yukl's (1989) definition of power relationship reinforces the idea that power is expressed in relationship, and the intent of the relationship is to modify the behavior or action of others. Power results from control over sources. Yukl's (1989) framework about power relationships in organizations enumerates three major types of power: position power, personal power, and political power.

Translated into teaching situations, a teacher entering her classroom has position power over students through a system of rewards/punishments (e.g., grading, assigning homework, calling parents if the student is misbehaving), ecological control (e.g., arranging and decorating the classroom according to her preferences; making decisions on time allocation for the different tasks, deciding on students who will be invited to respond), control over resources (such as materials for laboratory work or manipulatives for mathematics lessons), and control over information (such as direction coming from the principal, or mandates coming from district administrators).

Personal power is described in terms of personal characteristics, such as expertise, friendship (or care, as used by Noddings, 1984), and charisma. Translated into the education system, teacher experts seem to have power over the students. A perceived friendly attitude from the teacher can convince students to make the extra effort. Charismatic teachers (and I would add teachers who use humor while they are teaching – see also Ritchie et al., 2011; Roth et al., 2011) can have personal power over students who will go an extra step to please the teacher.

Political power is the result of controlling decision processes, developing coalitions, and gaining influence (Yukl, 1989) . An example of political power in a classroom situation is the instance when a "target" student helps the teacher move the lesson along by constantly paying attention and answering questions (e.g., the student in science and mathematics classes who sits in the first row, closest to the professor). These students tend to get recognized for their political power and receive higher grades, as "we know that they know the material because they answer all the questions verbally." An example of political power between teachers is demonstrated when a teacher says a comment like, "I had a lunch meeting with Jim [first name of the superintendent], and he clarified that..." However, the teacher neglects to indicate that more than 100 teachers also attended this meeting. A principal's use of political sources of power is exemplified through translating/interpreting directions from the district and denying teachers the right to have first-hand access to mandates; the principal is in a position of power given to her from knowing about, reading, and interpreting the original mandate (Foucault, 1979). Unfortunately, many teachers do not understand that they have the right to ask for the original document. Neither does the principal understand the implication that hiding [with or without intent] the original mandate from the teachers and implementing it without prior discussion results in no teacher "buy-in" to the new ideas.

In Moscovici (2003b) I develop three prototypes of teachers according to Yukl's categories of power: John – the dictator, Julie – the expert, and Steven – the political activist. John, the dictator, realizes that despite the "on task" behavior of his students in the classroom and compliments from the administration, his students' understanding of science is not being challenged and extended learned. Students recognize the teacher's sources of position power and want to get on his good side by following the rules. I recall many college science classes in which the professor did not appreciate being interrupted by student questions and, while still looking in his notes rather than facing the students, rhetorically asked "Are there any questions?. The focus of such teacher classes is delivery of prepared material rather than student learning (see also Professor Strauss, in Moscovici, 1994).

Julie, the "expert" teacher is student-oriented and wansts her chemistry students to become experts in researching and presenting findings. She does not follow the example of most college science teachers [and me, during my first three months of teaching] who use their expertise as legitimization to present students with the latest content discoveries without focusing on students' learning. I call these exhibitions of teacher centeredness—"let me show you what I know," "she knows so much," or "she is so intelligent"—an ode to the teacher.

Friesen (2011) provides us with the history behind the "lecture" style and the modernization of this form during the years. Use of newer media technologies with writing and oral communication has the potential to make lectures interactive (e.g., using discussion boards, Twitter). Of course, the choice of tools and the degree of interactivity are the professor's decision. The courses offered via television today – courses that allow high numbers of students to participate at the same time – have high enrollment. Even though the students are required to provide feedback on their peers' work (interactivity), the professor is unable to read and respond to students' comments, because of the large class size. Thus, students cannot take advantage of the expertise of the professor, and their thinking is not challenged. I have even seen lecture courses in which the professor used the same "let me show you what I know" style of teaching, whether she was teaching 250 or 10 students. The professor used the same techniques (overhead projector, short movies, and talking) and avoided interactions or interruptions of any kind (Moscovici, 1994). I also have observed a completely different style by a chemistry professor who used questioning strategies and group work to involve his 250 students in thinking and analyzing chemical data. He started with concrete examples and shifted to abstract chemical concepts (Singer & Moscovici, 2008), and students were more than willing to contribute to the discussions. The selection and use of available techniques is in the hands of the professor—still an exercise of personal power. The choice (and I believe the problem) is a matter of PCK (see below).

In Israel, part of my obligation as the parent president of the classrooms in which my children studied, was to fill "teacher of the day" – more like teacher for 30 minutes as none requested more time-slots with parents. I used my position power always to choose the vocal parents who did not appreciate the teachers and those who were always complaining. Despite their hours of preparation, these parents were not successful in their teaching, and students did not learn (a pattern which became apparent from studing students' responses on quizzes whose questions had been suggested the teaching parents). [we demonstrated this pattern using a short quiz with questions suggested by the teaching parents, according to their emphases]. Following their failure at the teaching experience, the "teaching" parents became the best supporters of the teachers. They learned that successful teaching required much more than just knowing the subject. Success required knowing pedagogy related to the subject, information about student learning styles and dispositions/intelligences (Gardner, 1983, 1991), and appropriate use of resources. Shulman (1986) named all the dimensions necessary for good teaching as "pedagogical content knowledge" or PCK. These dimensions include (but are not restricted to) content knowledge, pedagogical knowledge and knowledge about materials and equipment that facilitates student learning. Many researchers have studied the relationship between PCK and teaching and learning processes for both students and teachers (e.g., for science: Gess-Newsome & Lederman, 1999; for mathematics: Lampert, 1986; and in relation to Professional Learning Communities: Bausmith & Barry, 2011). Carroll and Mumme's (2011) seminar presentation in which they divide teachers' mathematical knowledge for teaching into mathematical content knowledge (including common content knowledge and specialized content knowledge) and PCK (including knowledge of content and teaching as well as knowledge of content) is especially interesting.

Teachers can develop and utilize political power in their classroom classroom. For example, Irene teaches her students the processes of science by having them measure the water quality in a lake near her elementary school. She plans a day in which students present posters displaying their data and understanding of the year long analysis of water quality. She invites parents and the group that funded her students' equipment. She involves the scientists who helped her teach the biology. She encourages reporters from the local news to report on the event. Through her planning and teaching during the school year, Irene has political power with her principal, grant funders, parents, and other teachers in her school. Another teacher, Steve, becomes the "political activist" with the principal by opening to visitors his well-organized classroom in which there are many students in special education. Visitors from local districts and parents see that the students enjoy themselves as they learn about the atom concept through other constructs (Roth et al., 2011). By helping the principal, Steve receives materials and equipment for his science classes, which ultimately serve his students.

As we know, the 21st century requires a different citizenry (The Partnership for the 21st Century Skills, 2006, 2009). We need to teach in a different way in order to develop active, independent, knowledgeable, and collaborative individuals, ready to compete in a global market. At the same time, we need to employ critical pedagogy and influence social change (McLaren & Kincheloe, 2007). We need to strive to become transformative intellectuals and discuss content issues and classroom norms with our students (Aronowitz & Giroux, 1993; Giroux & Simon, 1989) and use these experiences to learn and become better facilitators of learning (Moscovici, 2007).

Questions Set 4.3:

1. Recall an experience in which, despite the flow you felt during the teaching, students were not successful in understanding the concept. How did you find out? Write one to two paragraphs.
2. Analyze the situation in terms of power relationships. Which of Yukl's sources of power (1989) did you use (position, personal, or political)? How active were the students?
3. How could you modify the experience to enhance students' ability to learn?
4. As a group, record the different experiences in terms of power sources used. Do you see any patterns? Explore/explain the results as a group, or as a whole class.

A LAST WORD

Responsibility for Taking Action

As science and mathematics educators, we have the responsibility to grow professionally and better prepare our students to embrace successfully the challenges of the 21st century (The Partnership for 21st Century Skills, 2006, 2009). We must learn to use our knowledge of updated content, pedagogy, and the endless resources available today (Gess-Newsome & Lederman, 1999; Moscovici, 2007; Shulman, 1986). Once we know about situations that show inconsistencies and/or lack of equity, we need to deconstruct the situations, inconsistencies and/or inequities, and together with the students, think about possible solutions and consequences. As we weigh possibilities, we want to choose and implement the best solution (see also emotional literacy – e.g., Goleman, 1995). The idea is to become part of a changing world in which science and mathematics are subjects everybody understands and values (I would add loves, but I am not that courageous). Social justice and equal/equitable opportunities are a must as we create a world that supports emancipatory curriculum implementation (Anyon, 1980, 1997; Aronowitz & Giroux, 1993; Giroux & Simon, 1989; Grundy, 1987; McLaren & Kincheloe, 2007).

Masochistic Side of Teaching and the Requirements for Learning

Sometimes when I see our students struggling during the disequilibrium phase, I question our role as teachers. Lemke's (1990) thoughts regarding a teacher's right to ask students questions for which she already knows the answer comes to mind. We observe students surviving teacher questioning experiences in which the teacher monitors her questioning with pause points for specific scafflods. We must remember that the more one thinks, the more one learns. A teacher needs to ask students to think and find solutions, even if this role of facilitator or guide does not come easily, it is necessary. As *Homo sapiens*, students need to be encouraged to think and maximize their potential for wisdom and knowledge. We must be simultaneously involved in inquiery that related to improving the learning experience.

What can teachers bring to the classroom? They can:

1. Stretch beyond their potential as teacher and stretch students' potentials
2. Know about choices and consequences
3. Establish a collaborative and challenging teaching and learning environment – "if I don't learn, it is not worth teaching"
4. Move away from just presenting content expertise, "Let me show you what I know" (or teacher-centered) to PCK expertise: begin with where the students are, and let them solve first with scaffolds (no more than needed) – "move to show me what you know and let us learn together" (student-centered)

5. Know that "The more I, the teacher, say/think, the less they (students) say/think/learn"
6. Use Six Facets of Learning (Wiggins & McTighe, 1998: conceptual to procedural to metacognitive
7. Support verbal and written knowledge expressions
8. Use humor but not at students' expense
9. Scaffold but not give away the answers

As Whitehead (1967) writes in *The Aims of Education and Other Essays*:

It must never be forgotten that education is not a process of packing articles in a trunk... Its nearest analogue is the assimilation of food by a living organism: and we all know how necessary to health is palatable food under suitable conditions. When you have put your boots in a trunk, they will stay there till you take them out again; but this is not at all the case if you feed a child with the wrong food. (p. 33)

LEADERSHIP AS EFFECTIVE COLLABORATIONS IN SCIENCE AND MATHEMATICS

INTRODUCTION

This chapter looks at the variables in play during effective collaborations in science and mathematics and underscores the dynamics of success in leading 1) students in science and mathematics classrooms, 2) teachers in schools, and 3) teacher leaders at the district/state level. With the rise of specialization, we have abundant examples of experts from various fields (e.g., science/mathematics faculty, science/mathematics education faculty, school expert teachers, school administrators, district science/mathematics experts) joining forces in professional development sessions (Moscovici & Osisioma, 2009).

In a world with exponential knowledge growth, with more books and resources that we can read in a lifetime, what does it mean to lead? What are the necessary ingredients to be considered a leader? And how does one lead in a world in which information is readily available and technology is becoming increasingly more affordable and innovative? In order to answer to these questions, I will address the meaning of respect and trust among co-learners as well as the meaning of expertise. Needless to say that the concept of leadership has changed over time, and it is necessary to adapt to the new realities.

MY IDEA OF LEADERSHIP

It was not until an early work from the Association for Science Teacher Education (ASTE)-sponsored book edited by Wieseman and Weinburg (2009) that I thought about leadership in the science education community. Before then, I was involved in two large grants that looked at developing leadership in teachers' classrooms (teaching K-12), directing professional development activities (teaching adults), and guiding leaders' activities (learning to lead) (Loucks-Horsley, Love, Stiles, Mundry, & Heuson, 2003; Moscovici & Osisioma, 2009).

The idea of leadership layers is that while a teacher demonstrates leadership with her students, other layers of leaders attend to other populations: professional development leaders need to think about teachers and students, and leaders of leaders need to add the professional development of leaders and the teachers.

I am interested in exploring co-leadership models that work at different levels in every situation mentioned previously. While there is no question regarding a teacher's responsibility to lead students to learn and understand specific concepts

(Wiggins & McTighe, 1998 – the six facets of understanding), in a co-leadership model students need to decide or choose to become partners in the proposed or negotiated learning adventure or journey. As partners, students have the right to suggest alternatives, propose new ideas, and even challenge traditional ways in which things are done routinely (see the role of the transformative intellectual in Chapter 4 – Aronowitz & Giroux, 1993; Giroux & Simon, 1989). Once students' rights are accommodated, there are more chances for "buy into" implementation ("co-optation" as part of political power sources in Yukl, 1989) and joint responsibility for the final product:

> When someone is allowed to participate in making a decision, the person gains more influence over the decision but is also likely to become more committed to carry out the decision. Participation increases the total influence in the relationship rather than merely transferring some influence from the agent to the target person. The process illustrates the apparent paradox that you can gain more influence by giving up some influence, as long as the resulting decision is consistent with your objectives (Yukl, 1989, p. 27).

Van Sickle and Cudahy (2009) describe such leadership situations as "egalitarian" leadership (see also Ashkanasy, Trevor-Roberts, & Earnshaw, 2001) in which every participant's voice counts and the focus is on developing a learning community with equal distribution of power. As the "choir director," the leader needs to facilitate discussions, organize the experiences, and direct – meaning that the leader leads – participants in a certain direction.

At this stage of my discussion of leadership I call attention to an observation. While it might appear that the easiest part of leadership would be at the classroom level, personally, I think that it is the most difficult. The reason? It is mandatory for students to be in the classroom. At the other layers of leadership and adult learning in general, joining is more a matter of choice. As humans prefer to have choices instead of having to be in mandatory situations, I think it may be more difficult to earn the "buy into" with K-12 students who are required to attend school than with adults who choose to join a group (even though sometimes the principal, district personnel, etc. mandate the group's formation, as in the case of professional development).

While I like the "egalitarian leadership" model, I am slightly concerned about the implications of its name – "egal" meaning "=" or "equal" in Romanian. While the participants in an egalitarian leadership model have a say and the obligation to see that the proposed plan is carried out, the leader has some obligations/rights that extend beyond the participant level.

Using work done in the 1950s and 1960s, Yukl (1989) defines "participative leadership" to involve participants in decision-making processes. Yukl shows levels of participation along a continuum (Figure 5.1), which extends on the left labeled with no participation or influence by others (meaning participants) and autocratci decision making, and ends on the right with large influence by others and delegation of duties.

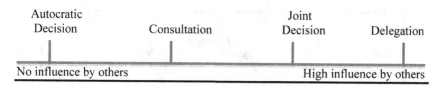

Figure 5.1. Yukl's continuum of decision procedures (Yukl, 2006, p. 83).

In my case, I use "consultation," "joint decision," and even "delegation" as examples of participative leadership. In addition, I use my Israeli background in leadership, which recognizes the fact that different individuals have various areas of expertise that a leader could tap into during training sessions. It also recognizes the contextual aspect of leadership and the fact that a leader in a certain situation could become a participant in another situation. Let me explain/elaborate on the dynamic of the Israeli leadership model.

When I arrived in Israel just months before the Yom Kippur War in 1973, I was in shock. Everybody used first names when addressing children or adults, even the prime minister. While trying to understand the high degree of familiarity or lack of formality, formality to which I was accustomed in Romania, I was told that status changed for each individual according to context and in order to diminish the confusion, first names were used. The example given was a CEO of a company who was recognized as a high level professional in the company, but who was transformed into a participant in a training session as part of the yearly army service, under the command of an 18-year old. In the civil context, the CEO would have a higher status, while in the army the 18-year old served as his boss. Using first names diminished the confusion. When I began teaching in secondary schools in Israel, students would use first names with their teachers. Furthermore, rather than separating ourselves from students by wearing professional clothing, we teachers would buy clothes paralleling youth fashion while also bearing in mind the adult professional Israeli teacher appearence. Very early in my teaching career I also learned that students in my classes were experts in many areas that I could use in classroom situations. For example, a student who helped his father in construction during summer months knew a lot about materials used in construction and their preparation. Another student was interested in electric current and wiring a house. I did not have any problem to switch my position from "classroom teacher (leader)" into "participant" when my students introduced their topics and used their expertise areas.

To summarize, I see myself using "participative leadership" in a dynamic way that encourages participants to share their expertise and add to the common learning experience (Figure 5.2). I also see the quality of the common learning experience as a direct result of the contribution of all the individual voices participating in the experience.

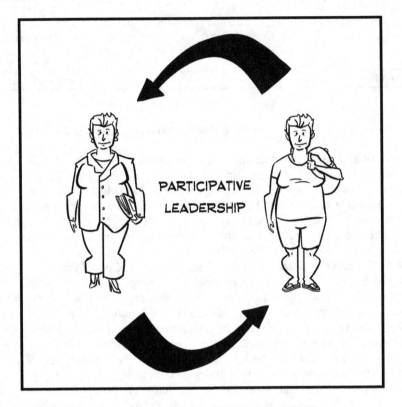

Figure 5.2. Hedy… using participative leadership.

LEADERSHIP EVENTS BEFORE SCHOOL – EARLY CHILDHOOD TIMES

When I think about the early period of my life before I attended school, two examples come to mind: leadership on the playground, and leadership in Jewish families. The first example relates to acting and achieving the best results in games among children, while the other looks at observing adult behavior and connecting actions and reasoning to outcomes.

Hide and Seek Followed by Switching Shoes

All the children in the neighborhood would gather for "hide and seek" games in our area, as there were many hiding places. Because of the dark buildings (Romania was trying to cut spending on electricity in areas with very low crime rate), we could just lie down and stand still on stairs or behind doors. Even the "seeker" when looking directly at us could not see our bodies. Sometimes we had to pay attention to breathing, as the possible noise of inhaling or the airflow from exhaling would give us away. The tension was excruciating.

Of course, with time we learned to close our eyes for a little while and experience darkness before trying to find the hidden children in dark buildings. We also learned to pretend that we saw the younger ones so that they would leave their hiding places or begin to laugh at jokes that we were telling while looking for them. However, the older children kept these secrets, and the younger ones had to pay their dues to learn this kind of knowledge.

Following "hide and seek" games, we would look for another challenge. In one of the buildings used for hide and seek there were many small apartments opening onto one side of a long corridor. As the individuals who lived there did not want to dirty their carpets, they would leave their shoes in the corridor at their doors. In our adrenalin rush, we would switch the shoes at the doors and run before any of the inhabitants reached their doors. The older children would lead the younger ones in this adventure, by sharing tips regarding keeping noise level down, avoiding bumping into each other, and increasing their running speed. Of course, following any bumping were cascades of laughter that increased the noise level and decreased the speed... but then, it was all part of the experience. The older children paid attention to adults entering the building and alerted the young ones of possible interferences (e.g., corridor inhabitants returning from work, shopping, or a night out).

On numerous occasions we were caught, and our parents received full reports of our nocturnal activities from the individuals displeased with switched shoes. A wide range of punishments followed our actions, from no punishment ("children will remain children" statements from parents who remembered their own childhood activities) to weeks of no outside play.

Jewish Family Dynamics

As mentioned previously, I have learned considerably about leadership by observing and understanding the rationale behind the behavior of individuals in Jewish families. As in most Jewish families, both my parents continued their education and became part of the intellectual middle class. My father served as an engineer for a large state company, "Nufar," which was involved in building gigantic textile cleaning facilities all over Romania. My mother became a pediatrician working for a clinic near Bucharest for a few years (part of "giving back" once getting her degree, at no personal cost in Socialist Romania). Following very difficult tests she was transferred to practice at a clinic in Bucharest. Both parents worked, and my grandma who was living with us was in charge of the house and the children, and cooked for us. During my sister's and my younger years, we also had a nanny who lived with us. Later, a house care person who came a few times per week replaced the nanny.

Children in my kind of Jewish family learned early that there is always a definite answer for some questions (e.g., always "no" for dating a non-Jewish boy, dating for a girl below age 16), while other questions have a less definite answer because of contextual factors. Let me explain:

I learned that trying to convince my father to let me go to a sleep-over (when I was young) or to a party on Friday night (when I was older) did not stand a chance if my attempts at convincing him took place in the evening when he came home hungry from work. Usually, these encounters ended up with a definitive "no." In order to change the "no" into a "yes," even a conditional yes (e.g., be home by midnight) I needed my mom's convincing powers. Once my mom agreed to help me, she knew how and when to bring the topic to my father and convince him to allow me to attend the party. She was able to convince him that it was his idea to let me do what he would have vetoed. She would also ask him to share "his" decision with me, as if he changed his mind. While I knew it was my mom's doing, I agreed to play the game and thanked my father for his reversed decision. Some might call this kind of behavior manipulation; however, it was a way of being that allowed both parents to have their powers recognized and valued.

Questions Set 5.1:

1. Do you recall a similar situation before school age in which you were in the position to lead, co-lead, or observe leadership at work? Write one to two paragraphs.
2. In small groups discuss similarities and differences between experiences shared and, as a group write one to two paragraphs summarizing these experiences. Use graphics if necessary or helpful.
3. Create a table of leadership experiences for the whole class and connect these to teaching science and/or mathematics.

LEADERSHIP EXPERIENCES RELATED TO SCIENCE AND MATHEMATICS DURING SCHOOL YEARS

In this section I focus on my learning experience with leadership during second grade when I became a pioneer in Socialist Romania and my high school experience in the special "Olympiad" chemistry/mathematics class for tenth and eleventh grades. Both experiences taught me that the other side of having rights is taking responsibility. In both experiences I was offered access to superior resources; however, I had responsibilities that came with these benefits.

Becoming a Pioneer in Socialist Romania

Along with the award of becoming a "pionier" or "pioneer" – for good grades and behavior in school as well as a written recommendation from Ms. Bayer, my second grade teacher – came rights and responsibilities. When I was finally allowed to enroll in courses offered at the "Casa Pionierului" in Bucharest and attend events that were offered only to the "pionier" group members, I felt all grown up. I was allowed to take the two buses to reach "Casa Pionierului," also known as "Palatul Pionierului" (pioneer's palace), attend courses such as general biology and folk dances from all over the world, and to return home, all on my own. As we attended these courses, the pioneers from different schools would interact and play, delaying our return home for as long as possible. Parents would be worried; however we were happy.

Together with rights came responsibilities. As pioneers, we were recognized as very good students in academics and behavior, and as such we served as unofficial helpers to the teacher. We were the ones showing and explaining how to solve difficult mathematics problems on the blackboard, helping a student with class work, or making sure a sick classmate arrived home and that an adult was there to take care of her needs. Early on we (pioneers) learned that together with rights (e.g., taking advantage of enrichment programs offered free of charge in academic as well as sports areas) came responsibilities (e.g., helping other students in class who experienced difficulties). We also learned that helping students with mathematics problem-solving was not easy, especially as Ms. Bayer did not allow us to show them how to solve the problem, but had us help the student reach the necessary understanding to be able to explain to Ms. Bayer how to solve it.

As part of our pioneer responsibility and to support Ms. Bayer's effort to convince classmates to become pioneers, we had to prepare presentations on what we did at the "Casa Pionierului" and even show materials, when possible. I recall carrying a heavy glass container with a creature in formalin as part of my show. I was very proud to be trusted with such a precious item, and I knew all about the creature and the preservation procedure.

High School Olympiad Classes

After a year of focusing on academics during ninth grade in single gender classes in a bi-gender high school, the counselors called the students to choose areas of study for the remainder of high school - tenth, eleventh, and twelfth grades. As I had very good grades in mathematics and science subjects and teacher recommendations, I could choose between the "Olympiad" mathematics or chemistry classes. The "Olympiad" classes offered enhanced studies in one area of emphasis and other related subjects at the highest level. For example, choosing the chemistry option meant that we had to study mathematics at the highest level.

The chemistry option class consisted of only 23 students who received personal attention; we could not hide behind other students as in a class of 40. Part of our responsibility was to solve problems appearing in the Olympiad journals for chemistry and for mathematics, as well as to propose problems to be reviewed and hopefully be published in these journals. With our extremely busy schedules, my classmates and I realized that we needed to work together in order to survive, as alone a student could not be successful in all the required tasks. We (the students) joined forces, and, according to strengths, divided the work. Together we decided on deadlines, meeting times and places, and the number of problems to be solved and/or invented. In case of unforeseen challenges such as difficulty solving a problem in one of the journals, we would readdress the issue during class breaks since we stayed together in the same classroom. Classmates also had the responsibility to explain in depth their problem-solving technique because we all had to participate in the yearly Olympiad competitions for high school chemistry and mathematics.

In Romania during those times (1970s) students stayed in regular classrooms and teachers moved from one classroom to another. Such a setting encouraged communication and collaboration among students. Exceptions to this rule were the laboratory classes, such as in chemistry (each science branch had their own laboratory with special furniture, equipment, and materials).

Looking back, I can say that participative peer leadership in science and mathematics helped my peers and me to survive the pressure and high expectations of the Olympiad chemistry class. The experience also prepared me to organize and participate in productive group work – necessary skills for success in the sciences.

Questions Set 5.2:

1. Can you recall similar situations during your formal schooling that involved leadership in science or mathematics classes? Write one to two paragraphs describing the experience and the relationship between leader and participants.
2. In small groups discuss similarities and differences between shared experiences, and, as a group, write one to two paragraphs summarizing these experiences. Use graphics if necessary or helpful.
3. Create a table of leadership experiences for the whole class and connect these to leadership styles in science and/or mathematics classrooms.

LEADERSHIP MODELS AND IDEAS

Before addressing a fraction of the literature on leadership that I have read and utilized, I want to explore my realization that despite the fact that I was not seeing myself as a leader, others did. Colleagues from the university, science educators at conferences, science experts and specialists in the local school districts, school district administrators—all acknowledged my expertise in science, mathematics, and science education, as well as the ideas that I had concerning what I would like to see in science and mathematics classrooms when supervising interns or student teachers. What I considered tutoring and sharing, others considered leadership (see also Kaser, Mundry, Styles & Loucks-Horsley, 2006, p. 3, entitled, "We Are All Leaders").

Me, a Leader?

As mentioned earlier in this chapter, I first looked at myself as a leader in 2005 when I was invited by Katherine Wieseman, a friend, co-author, and colleague in science education, to participate in leadership sessions offered at the annual meetings of ASTE (then known as Association for the Education of Teachers of Science) and NARST—A Worldwide Organization for Improving Science Teaching and Learning Through Research (Wieseman et al., 2005a & 2005b). These sessions focused on challenges encountered by women trying to balance academic/professional work with their personal lives (Figure 5.3).

Figure 5.3. Balancing acts—personal and professional lives.

At one of these leadership sessions Uri Zoller, a well known chemistry educator from Israel added that women were not the only ones to encounter these challenges, but all professionals may appreciate and take part in both areas simultaneously (e.g., answering to the demands of academia and advancing through the ranks while fully participating in raising a family). These conference sessions led to the development of the book entitled, *Women's Experiences in Leadership in K-16 Science Education Communities: Becoming and Being,* edited by Wieseman and Weinburgh (2009), and published with the sponsorship of ASTE.

Since 2002 I have been involved in the brainstorming and later the development of two major grants involving the Los Angeles Unified School District (LAUSD) and California State University – Dominguez Hills where I served on the faculty: 1) *System-wide Change of All Learners and Educators* (SCALE) grant, an NSF-supported endeavor to change the way science and mathematics entered classrooms in different school districts in the USA, and 2) *Quality Educator Development* (QED) grant, a California Department of Education project to continue the work of SCALE locally (LAUSD teachers and students) with neighboring universities, such as California State University – Northridge and California State University – Los Angeles. In the SCALE grant I was part of the Immersion Task Force that developed science investigations for science students, which integrated grade-appropriate science standards following the features of inquiry as explored in *Inquiry and the National Science Education Standards,* published by the NRC (2000). For the QED grant I served as the lead person for the science team. Still, the idea of me as a leader had not entirely clicked for me.

In the 2005-2006 academic year, I was part of a Los Angeles team sent to a Leadership Academy for Mathematics and Science organized by WestEd. The four face-to-face sessions, as well as the work between the sessions, readings, discussions, and final presentation enhanced my knowledge about ways to organize and work with others, including being a considerate, but also task-oriented leader.

It is hard to say when I realized that I was a leader, other than it happened sometime between 2002 and 2008. However, I still had a long process in defining *my* leadership style. While I was trying to do so, I found many different literature texts that focused on leadership in science and mathematics, as well as on leadership with specific populations, (e.g., teachers, individuals in the business community, or large organizations).

Leadership Models and Ideas

I am amazed at the number of publications on the topic of leadership – for this reason I consider my examination of the topic in this book to be the tip of an iceberg. While I cite publications on leadership in science and mathematics, I also address some theories not directly developed for these fields, as the theories offer interesting perspectives or schemas.

For me, the most influential author on leadership has been Yukl (1989), especially as he explores the sources of power available to a leader and the implications of the use of power. Yukl (1989, p. 84) looks at the continuum of power sharing in participative leadership in organizations (Figure 5.1). Yukl's description for "Joint Decision" as "the manager has no more influence over the final decision than any other participant," is reminiscent of the "egalitarian model" for leadership (Ashkanasy, 2001; Van Sickle & Cudahy, 2009). Yukl clarifies the difference between true participation and pretense. In the case of pretense, the manager may solicit ideas from others, however, ignores other's suggestions in the decision. I would add from my personal experience in school systems and academia that sometimes a decision is already made; however, in order to diminish possible outbursts from displeased workers, a meeting is held to permit voicing opinions.

Big Dog and Little Dog (2010) use a survey to identify leadership style. Their leadership categories are similar to those of Yukl (1989), as they both use the level of participation in decision-making as the overarching criterion. Big Dog and Little Dog define three categories of styles of leadership: authoritarian (autocratic), participative (democratic), and delegative (free reign).

Glanz modifies Null's Natural Life Energy theory framework (see Null, 1996 in Glanz, 2002; Glanz, 2012) written for educators. Glanz (2002, 2012) offers a matrix of seven quality types of natural leadership (p. 7) consisting of:

1) Dynamic/Aggressive
2) Dynamic/Assertive
3) Dynamic/Supportive
4) Adaptive/Aggressive
5) Adaptive/Assertive
6) Adaptive/Supportive
7) Creative/Assertive

Glanz clarifies, "All of us, of course, possess a degree of each quality. At times, all of us can demonstrate creativity, assertiveness, and even dynamism. Again, the point is that each of us has a dominant natural quality" (p. 6). For each quality type, Glanz offers a continuum of personal characteristics from "low" (focus on self) to "high" (focus on others), and detailed explanations and examples. Glanz's Appendix A offers a survey aimed at finding one's personal leadership type. Glanz (2002) also defines the virtues that every leader needs to have: courage, impartiality, empathy, judgment, enthusiasm, humility, and imagination (see also Glanz, 2003). For example, my leadership type using Glanz' survey of 56 questions combines Dynamic/Assertive with 7/8 votes with Creative/Assertive and Dynamic/Supportive, each with 6/8 votes. What does this mean? According to Glanz, I am an innovator, as well as a designer and a healer. Of course, I also need to pay attention to the low end of each category to avoid thinking of myself first during leadership activities.

In another text, written for teachers, Glickman (2002) defines four types of teachers according to two axes intersecting at each axis' midpoint (similar to a plus sign), thus creating four quadrants. The y-axis is Level of Abstraction [ability to find patterns in data and reach conclusions and provide recommendations]; the x-axis is Level of Commitment [to clients – students in this case] (p. 88). Teachers in Quadrant IV (top right) exhibit high levels of abstraction and commitment to students, and are the desired category of "Professionals."

Also emphasizing the importance of data analyses, Love, Styles, Mundry and DiRanna (2008) suggest that engaging individuals who are stakeholders in collaborative inquiry, and using data coaches and data teams to analyze pertinent data and reach decisions, will improve all students' results. In their conceptualization, collaborative inquiry serves as a bridge with *Data* on the left side of the bridge and *Results* on the right side of the bridge. The bridge of collaborative inquiry has four components: 1) leadership and capacity; 2) collaboration; 3) data use; and 4) instructional improvement, all four embedded in a context of culture/equity/trust (p. 18).

English (2008) in his text, *The Art of Educational Leadership,* develops an elegant table (5.1 on pp. 136–137) connecting the needs of the followers, tasks of the leader, and aspects of the leader's performance. As we all know, it is important to identify and answer the needs of the participants as a way to lower the potential rise in negative energy due to unmet needs. Of course, sometimes needs can be discussed in terms of data sources and collaborative inquiries, as described in Love et al. (2008).

Taking a cultural approach to leadership, Ashkanasy (2001) identifies certain characteristics of a leader in the "Anglo cluster" that comprises seven countries: Australia, Canada, England, Ireland, New Zealand, South Africa (white sample), and the USA. These characteristics are charismatic, team-oriented, and participatory.

In conclusion, there are certain requirements for a leader (e.g., commitment to clients and ability for abstraction – see Glickman, 2002); also, there are various leadership styles as well as differences among the participants. Acknowledging both leadership styles and participants' needs improves a leadership situation and provides for better chances of implementation and use. As *Homo sapiens*, we need to be aware of our beliefs and actions, evaluate the effects of our exploits, and improve the quality of our experiences for future implementations.

School as the minimal unit for change

In leadership in science and mathematics areas, I should mention the works of Gamoran et al. (2003), Loucks-Horsley et al. (2003), and the text, *Women's Experiences in Leadership in K-16 Science Education Communities: Becoming and Being,* edited by Wieseman and Weinburgh (2009). The first two publications emphasize the need to focus on the school as the smallest unit for change (similar to Cunningham & Cordeiro 2006; Glanz, 2011; Hall & Hord, 2006; Huber, 2004; Perez et al., 2007; Seyfarth, 2008), and the use of participative leadership or collaborative leadership as called by Glanz (2011) in his 2005 book entitled *What Every Principal Should Know About Collaborative Leadership.* This kind of leadership encourages a bridge between research and practice by using student learning and other data to set goals related to critical issues, planning and using accepted strategies, and evaluating results leading to revisions to the whole process of reform (Loucks-Horsley et al., 2003, p. 18). As in all system-based reforms, success depends on full cohesion and support from all stakeholders. Taking a global perspective, Huber states: "In many countries, the efforts made to improve schools have illustrated that neither top-down measures alone nor the exclusive use of bottom-up approaches have the effects desired. Instead, a combination and systematic synchronization of both has proved most effective" (p. 670). In other words, participatory leadership seems to work in situations in which experts and novices are changing according to the specific situation at hand. This participatory leadership must be in place for all stages of change, from establishing goals, to designing ways to achieve them, evaluating results and making necessary modifications to ensure students' success in general, and in science and mathematics in particular (see also Moscovici, 2009).

When discussing whole school improvement, we shift from just science and mathematics, or just individual teachers to a larger arena that encourages cohesion, focus, and collaboration among all sectors of schooling. A remarkable resource from the American Institutes for Research (2007) entitled *Successful California Schools in the Context of Educational Adequacy,* emphasizes the elements that contribute to successful schools, despite the disadvantages of the populations they serve. What really struck me in this report was the difference in attitudes of members of the teaching and administrative groups from schools that were failing compared to schools that were "beating the odds." In failing schools the attitude was "give me materials, money, help" as opposed to a "give me another year or two and we are going to reach our goals in schools beating the odds." In the area of literacy, Reeves (2005) finds that successful schools focus on students' areas of struggle in learning, performance-based assessments to evaluate student progress, and student work as data for discussions.

Co-leading

In order to ensure full participation of all sectors involved in school change, it is imperative to build teams with representatives from all sectors, teams that will serve in leadership roles (Moscovici, 2009). While we all understand the need to collaborate for the common goal (student success/student improvement), we all have our sociocultural backgrounds and contexts in which we function everyday. Leading at the science classroom level (Kitonga, 2010), leading at the school level (Gamoran, et al., 2003), or leading leaders at the district/state level (Moscovici & Osisioma, 2009), we are all influenced by the sociocultural milieu in which we were born and raised, as well as the different contexts in which we learned to function. Adjusting and negotiating are a must in order to become a voice that is heard and able to add to the conversation.

Although all the resources used for the leadership literature touch on the development of a "co-culture" of collaboration, to use Jandt's (2007) term, I find the works of Garmston and Wellman (1999), Garmston (2000a, 2000b), and Jandt (2007) essential for successful co-leading. While Garmston (2000a, 2000b) and Garmston and Wellman's works (1999) focus on collaborative leadership at the school/organizational level, Jandt (2007) introduces us into intercultural communication in today's global community (Kitonga, 2010; Moscovici & Osisioma, 2009).

Garmston and Wellman (1999) emphasize the need for developing seven collaborative norms that will accompany group members during collaboration. These norms include: 1) pausing; 2) paraphrasing; 3) probing for specificity; 4) putting ideas on the table; 5) paying attention to self and others; 6) presuming positive intentions; and 7) pursuing a balance between advocacy and inquiry. The norms focus on the need to comprehend and address other points of view during discussions, and to be flexible while inquiring into the personal positions of others.

Looking at the different types of co-presenting or co-leading, Garmston (2000a) elaborates on five types: 1) tag-team with presenters taking turns; 2) speak-and-comment when one presenter makes a statement while the other adds/comments; 3) speak-and-chart in which presenter leads while the support person charts/records comments; 4) perform-and-comment in which one presenter is on stage while the other focuses the audience's attention to following the important piece, and 5) duet with presenters showing total familiarity with each other and the subject so that they can finish each other's sentences. Co-presenting includes co-planning, requiring alignment of basic beliefs on teaching, learning, and working together among collaborators. In addition, the co-presenters need to develop trust, help the others look good, and be able to lend a hand in case of need. Respect for the ability of co-presenters to fill in for one another is also a trait of those who are successful.

As an example of co-development, co-presenting, and co-evaluating I refer to Moscovici and Osisioma (2009). Moscovici had already worked with district science specialists and lead science teachers, and, because of that, knew their beliefs regarding professional development preparation processes, as well as their debriefing and evaluation protocols in use. While university faculty needed to be identified at least weeks in advance to attend/collaborate in a meeting or a professional development activity, district science employees functioned in a 24-hour time frame. In addition, and because of the narrow time window, district people were less open to discussion and analysis of various options, and instead looked for a voice proposing an idea and ways of implementing the idea. These beliefs led to a cultural conflict with Osisioma, whose ways of interaction differed tremendously from the district partners. Establishing norms of collaboration served as an invaluable tool to begin developing a culture of co-collaboration and co-leading, a culture in which all voices were respected and valued, and in which individuals moved smoothly from being experts to becoming learners: i.e., professional leaders of the leaders community.

Moving into the global arena, Moscovici and Varella (2007) report on co-leading professional development sessions with teachers and science and/or mathematics leaders in Armenia, Romania, and Israel, and compare these experiences with those of their U.S. counterparts. The two researchers reported two major findings: 1) School teachers and administrators served as part of the co-leadership teams (ensuring a balance between globalization and local identity – see Singer, 2007) and as participants in all countries, except teachers from the USA who served only as participants, and 2) Professional development sessions in all countries involved in this study required participants to partially pay for their experience. Only U.S. teachers received stipends for attending professional development sessions and the union support this activity.

Questions Set 5.3:

1. Recall a leadership situation, which according to you, resulted in a total disappointment. Write one to two paragraphs.
2. Analyze the situation in terms of leadership models (e.g., Glanz' 2002 seven leadership styles; Glickman's 2002 model with Commitment and Abstraction axes; Yukl's 1989 levels of participative leadership) and, when the leadership involved more than one presenter/leader, collaboration levels.
3. Looking at participants' learning and any resulting improved student learning, how would you modify the leadership situation to increase the effect of the leadership situation on these elements?
4. In small groups, discuss the leadership situations, literature, and possible modifications to improve the experience. Are any patterns emerging?
5. As a whole group, share group patterns and create a table representing whole group results and learning.

WHO NEEDS SCIENCE AND MATHEMATICS?[3]

INTRODUCTION

This chapter attempts to answer the question of who needs science and mathematics, a question which repeatedly appears and is asked in science and mathematics classrooms. Although individuals of all ages use concepts and principles from science and mathematics in their everyday life, during their schooling years, they do not seem to make the connection between school science and mathematics and everyday life. While I am hesitant to label prenatal behavior as thinking, I am convinced that after birth, *Homo sapiens* begins to collect information about herself as well as the world around her -- to think, feel, and act in inextricably intertwined ways (Damasio, 1999). With the passage of years, the *Homo sapiens'* life experiences accumulate and the challenges increase in difficulty. Thus she needs more sources of information to make sense of herself and her world, and to confront challenges as they appear. She needs a more sophisticated system to process information, draw conclusions, and make choices based on her conclusions.

In this chapter, in order to respond to the question of who needs science and mathematics, I offer examples of everyday need for knowledge of science and mathematics. The first examples feature instances experienced by individuals during early childhood years. Subsequent examples relate to situations that children during the elementary school years and youth during the secondary school years may encounter. The examples are from my experiences as a mother. The final example, which shares aspects of my story with ovarian cancer, I believe, offers the ultimate challenge to humanity.

SCIENCE AND MATHEMATICS AS TOOLS TO BE INFORMED CONSUMERS

I invite you to think of science and mathematics knowledge like tools needed for engaging in life and making sense of life experiences. We need these tools to know the possibilities in the world and our limits. Our knowledge leads us to answers and an array of solutions, from which we may make choices as informed individuals and consumers in today's society.

As an example, I have a craving for one of my favorite meals, meatballs with tomato sauce and breadsticks. Instead of going to a restaurant or buying premade meatballs with sauce and breadsticks from a grocery store, I like to make the meal myself, and so recipes offer me answers for my culinary craving. The journey begins with appropriate proportions of raw materials like ground meat, rice, spices, flour, yeast, salt, and water. By reading the recipe's directions I know the ingredients that have to be mixed, the order of mixing, the temperatures needed for chemical reactions to occur, and the time for cooking – cooked meatballs and fully baked bread sticks. A delicious, mouth-watering meal! When I use the recipes I take full advantage of someone's mathematics and science knowledge of chemistry (proportions, chemical reactions, and temperature and pressure relationships) as tools for my own experience. Without this knowledge I might experience a horrible stomachache from uncooked dough. The mathematics and science knowledge in the form of recipes are tools, presenting me with known answers from which I can make choices. If I disregard the recipes' content or if no recipes are available, then I rely on my existing mathematics and science knowledge, and experience with the science of foods, taste and flavor, and kitchen chemistry, and the mathematics of quantities, proportions, and shapes. I experiment with quantities and proportions, and heating temperatures, and discover the process that results in the best preparation and flavors. As an individual and consumer with a need, and according to my personality and preferences, I make choices. Knowledge acts as a tool that a person can use in everyday situations as she makes choices in her life.

I illustrate in the above example the interconnectedness of mathematics and science. Can you think of instances of science divorced from mathematics? I cannot. The understanding of the ways our human body functions offers many examples of the interdependence of science and mathematics, such as: blood flow through vessels of differing diameters, rates of digestion as a result of different food combinations, and movement in various directions in an efficient and coordinated way. Using the technology that pervades our lives requires that it functions properly, for example, an airplane successfully lifting off a runway, unbroken conversation on one's cellular phone while riding as a passenger in a car traveling at the speed limit through a rural area. Otherwise we have to engage in a different set of decisions in a trouble-shooting, problem-solving mode, for example: electronic files lost because the computer operating system crashed and files had not been backed up.

Being a citizen in the global 21st century society and addressing and resolving complex problems, many of which stem from activities of our own creation, requires using knowledge and skills, which were not necessary for successful living in previous centuries. The Partnership for the 21st Century Skills (2006) and the NSTA (2011) lists' of skills include: subject knowledge such as 1) science and mathematics as academic subjects and as integrated into everyday life; 2) information, media and technology skills; 3) adaptability; creativity and innovativeness; 4) non-routine problem solving; 5) interpersonal skills; 6) high morality; and, 7) work ethics. Based on my understanding of living and learning as a cognitive and emotional activity, I add 8) emotional intelligence and 9) literacy (Goleman, 1995; Matthews, 2004, 2005) to the list of 21st century skills.

Being a 21st century global citizen also requires that, because she is a consumer in society, *Homo sapiens* comprehends messages and arguments discussed in the media. The educated and informed consumer must see beyond the distracting blur techniques used by a savvy media community to influence and sway consumer thinking and decision-making. She needs to know the process of checking for accuracy of information, and make her own decisions. Mathematics and science knowledge can serve as tools for recognizing media persuasive strategies and for sorting through the blur to interpret and evaluate information. *Homo sapiens* uses these tools to differentiate fact from personal bias, from elements that might be known but not be being told, or those essential to know but being de-emphasized or ignored. Knowing, thinking about our knowledge, and awareness of our own emotional dimension lead us to be able to make informed choices (Figure 6.1).

Figure 6.1. Informed citizen translating media blur.

EVERYDAY SCIENCE AND MATHEMATICS BEFORE SCHOOL ERA – EARLY CHILDHOOD TIMES

Since birth we explore the world around us. By using our mouth, head and neck muscles we begin to taste all that is within reach. Changes in light intensity and patterns catch our eyes' gaze, and we use head and neck muscles to turn our faces to study objects that have captured our curiosity. Sounds have a similar effect on our ears, and thus our orientation in space. Through sight and sound cues we learn to recognize individuals who are important in our lives, such as parents and siblings, and we learn to demand attention.

A baby crying in her crib is likely immediately to bring a nearby adult to the scene, and the adult just as quickly tries to resolve the problem that led to the baby's discontent. The solution often takes place by the adult lifting the crying baby from the crib and holding her in an embrace that communicates a sense of caring, warmth and safety. In this process, the baby makes the connection between her crying and an adult coming to her rescue - cause and effect, or stimulus and response. As the early years pass, we learn to crawl, stand, walk, skip and run as ways to explore our world. The science and mathematics of the senses and movement and motion are essential tools in these early explorations.

In order to address this topic, I share three stories from my early years of motherhood. The stories point out that although many pathways for learning exist, the personal direct experience is often the most prevalent one in the early years. As a mother I would learn by listening to the stories of other adults, but it was from direct experience with my sons' reactions that I discovered their true wants and needs. I learned that my eldest son favored learning through direct experience and inductive reasoning, while my middle son learned from listening. The stories are ones of sensory experiences with the science and mathematics of free-fall physics; properties of water; heat and temperature-pressure relationships; nutrition, taste, and digestion; and chemical reactions. They involve experiences with cause-effect (stimulus-response) relationships, and exchange and interdependence. The stories illuminate cognition-emotion connections.

Experiences with Free Fall Physics

As the first example, when my eldest son Danny was seven months old, he was not sitting properly. Gil, his friend, could stand and move around. Danny knew when Gil would be visiting because we would take out pillows, put Danny on the floor, and surround him with pillows so he would not fall over when Gil was freely moving around him. When Gil would appear, Danny would curl up in a ball because he knew that Gil would bump and push him with his leg. Danny used his science and mathematics knowledge of free fall physics for protection. This story also shows the different developmental rates in children, and that faster or slower rate is not good or bad. It is just different.

First Experiences with the Transformation of Water

As a second example, I recall when Uri would prepare the bath water for the boys' first experiences with water in the baby tub. He wanted to be sure that the water temperature would not shock their systems - not too hot or too cold. He knew the correct temperature by dipping his elbow into the tub water. He would estimate just the right amount of water so the depth was not too deep to frighten them and not too shallow that it was impossible to cup the water and flow it over their small bodies. Uri used science knowledge about sensory receptors, the nervous system and neuroscience, and mathematics knowledge of proportions to create a safe and pleasurable environment for our boys' first lessons with water.

Early water experiences also relate to biological needs and eating preferences. Adults would tell us not to feed the boys before bathing them so they would not puke, but our sons would cry and fret when we did this. They did not like baths before eating. They preferred eating first - they were hungry. They never puked in the bathwater. Also they wanted nothing with burping when the adult thought they were done feeding. They learned quickly that burping meant the meal was done, and they did not want someone else determining when a meal was done. They wanted both breasts and later the bottle (water in a different form) for as long as they wanted. This story about feeding (and water in at least three transformations) shows that choices and decisions happen from birth – even babies can be informed consumers for matters important to them. Hunger is a primary biological need and it has emotional and learning implications. Remember Maslow's Hierarchy of Needs? We recognize these implications in schooling by providing programs such as free and reduced meal programs, because we know that we cannot learn at our optimum if we are hungry.

Water was first part of the boys' life experiences in the forms of bath water, breast milk and liquids in bottles, and later as shower water and pool water. I was told that young children often did not like showers, so when we went to the university pool in Jerusalem three times weekly, I would hold them on my breast and playfully show them that shower water was just water, something they already knew about from bath water. When we were in the swimming pool we would play games with the water by pooling, blocking and gently splashing the water. We have a human ability to transform the meaning of water to anything we want it to mean, depending on ways we choose to use it. Water is an essential ingredient in drinks (like breast milk) needed for survival. It can become water for cleansing (bathwater and shower water) to which young children can relate through play. As pool and salty seawater, it can become a place for enjoyment, exercise and relaxation from stress, as children and adults immerse themselves. Under some circumstances, like a near drowning experience, the human emotional response with water might not be so pleasurable; it might be painful. The science and mathematics of water is a story about transformation in the meaning of a ubiquitous substance (a liquid that is often cold, to something enjoyed and loved) and a pleasure-pain emotional response through observation and inquiry. It is a story rich with decision-making and consumer choices, for the well being of the individuals involved.

Cause-Effect and the Mathematics of Economics

As a last point in the discussion of everyday use of science and mathematics during early childhood, I relate a third story from my years as a young mother living in Israel. In Israel, 12 weeks after the birth of a child the parents have to return to work. We found our solution to this childcare (consumer) problem in the home of a loving Moroccan woman with three children of her own. She had been told that she could not have any more children; the science of human reproduction turned into a tragedy for her. Raising our children with her own children helped her with this tragedy, and the arrangement became an opportunity for economic exchange and interdependence. The six children (hers and ours) would play together during the days when my husband and I were working. This was an advantage for the children's socialization, and besides that, our children would not be left alone.

On Thursdays she would make a cheese bourekas (a kind of pastry which the Russians call pirogi). The boys loved bourekas. From the minute he could walk, my eldest son Danny would go stand in front of the oven and wait for the bourekas to be ready. In the beginning he burned his hand from touching the hot oven, and from this stimulus-response experience, he learned to associate oven with hot and pain. After that experience he patiently would wait because he knew that the bourekas were in the oven and eventually would be taken out. After that experience he would take me to the oven in our home, point to it, and in Hebrew say, "hot." This story points again to a cognition-emotion connection – the pleasure of eating bourekas versus the pain from having been burned. The feeling of hunger and a food connection provides an impetus for learning, this time in a context of reward being something worth waiting for rather than "I'm hungry, feed me, nothing else matters." The reward and pleasure of eating something one likes, reminds me of an often-used (food bribery) classroom management practice of sweets as treats for good behavior.

Questions Set 6.1:

1. What experiences from your early years in life do you remember? What were you doing?
2. Form pairs and share your memories of these experiences. Together brainstorm aspects of science and mathematics that might be related to your experiences. For example, movement/motion, forces, human respiration, sensory organs, muscles, shape recognition, counting, curiosity, exploration, discovery, reasoning, cause-effect relationship, observation, estimation, measurement, and inference.
3. Create a table listing activities in which children ages 0-5 years might engage and record relevant science and mathematics concepts and/or skills for these activities.

EVERYDAY SCIENCE AND MATHEMATICS DURING FORMAL SCHOOLING – ELEMENTARY

From an early age, as children we become consumers. With money in our pockets, we accompany older individuals and friends to stores to decide ways to spend our pocket money. To be a sophisticated and informed consumer today one must be clever. For example, one must be knowledgeable when reading product labels in order to determine the best buy because companies demonstrate equal cleverness by playing into human desires and wants (different from human survival needs), by pricing items a few cents below a whole dollar amount, presenting information using different unit systems and using technical (for many consumers a foreign) language in listing product ingredients. The mathematical cognitive demand on a young consumer is much higher today than in the past because today's youth have money in their pockets and the media invades every aspect of daily existence through television, radio, Internet, magazines, advertisements and signs. The scientific cognitive demand also is much higher today than in the past because the language of science can be a foreign language to the uninformed consumer.

During the years associated with elementary schooling we learn ways to stay clean and be healthy, and physically and emotionally safe. Parents persuade, coerce or require us to bathe and brush our teeth for the two minutes currently recommended by dentists. They teach us personal hygiene routines and enforce sleep schedules to reduce the frequency of succumbing to illness like colds, flu and diarrhea. Family members, fearful for their children's safety, may insist "do not talk to strangers," and teach their young children to use a cell phone so they know where they are at all times. Through the parent-child relationship (facial expressions, body language, paralinguistic cues like voice tone, word choice) children learn early lessons about violence between humans and bullying, a pattern of human relationships, receiving great attention in schools today.

Outside the family setting a child trying to cross a busy road with no crosswalk is likely to draw the attention of a nearby older individual who offers to help. In order to cross safely, the individual might model looking in all directions and estimating the time available to cross the street in relation to vehicle's speed. Science and mathematics knowledge related to the interdependence of human body systems, conceptions of health and wellbeing, environmental awareness, geometry and vectors, force interactions, and biomechanics are essential tools in these experiences.

A Passion for Being in Water

Like me, my three sons, have a passion for being in the water. Their passion evolved from the early experiences and pleasures of playing with shower water to swimming and playing in saltwater, to eventually becoming accomplished surfers of ocean waves.

When we lived in Israel, the family visited Eilat on the Red Sea, a resort area at the southernmost tip of Israel. Sunny skies blanket the warm and crystal seawaters. As a result of the temperate gulf water temperatures, Eilat has amazing sea life - fish and coral reefs. Yearly, the migration routes between Europe and Africa take millions of birds through Eilat. Here I watched the boys become interested in floating on water. They would stand on anything, any piece of wood that they could find. We also visited the beaches on the Mediterranean Sea, where my sons started riding the waves and learned to manipulate their bodies and small boards so the waves would carry them to shore.

When Danny was twelve, Tal seven and Ido (the youngest) three years old, we moved from Israel to Tallahassee in the state of Florida, USA, where I pursued doctoral studies in science education at Florida State University. Early during our years in Florida, my youngest son Ido would ask which was his house, because according to him we were traveling all the time. In Florida we lived about an hour's drive from the Gulf of Mexico and though I was very busy as a doctoral student, we spent weekends at the Gulf. We walked on the beach, and played and swam in the water. My husband would go fishing because he loved to fish in any body of water, and he taught the boys how to fish. I would bake the fish they caught.

Every year until my sons finished high school we would take water-related holiday trips. First there were trips within Florida, then Niagara Falls in New York, and Lake Tahoe in California. These water and travel experiences were seeds for later studies and adult passions, like Danny's initial idea to pursue university studies in marine biology and his ultimate decision for a bachelor's degree in travel and tourism with a minor in recreation. As an adult he chooses to live near the ocean surf, so that each morning he can watch the energy of the waves, tides, and wind as his weather forecast. He may feel sick when he heads with his surfboard into the surf, but on the board, he feels less sick. Surfing is not only a passion; it is a spiritual practice. He also uses sea kayaks, and using a snorkel, he dives to see the aquatic life. He notices seasonal and annual changes in water patterns and currents, kelp growth and ocean life in relation to La Niña and El Niño currents. From observing, he has learned that shark attacks may be more likely during red tides (scientists call them harmful algal blooms), since the higher plankton blooms bring small fish close to shore, which in turn, draw in sharks. Though a great time for fishing, fish caught then should not be eaten because one might ingest the algae producing the toxins, and get sick.

Responding to our passion for water required constantly using everyday science and mathematics knowledge to ensure that we were physically safe and felt emotionally safe when we were near and in the water. The slope of the beach needed to be not too steep or else we would lose our footing, water currents pulling us away from the beach not too strong so that we would be able to return to shore, wave height and action not too strong to knock us down, and water temperature not too cold to take away our breath. We needed to be aware of jellyfish floating nearby not to be stung with resulting welts or an even stronger allergic reaction. Our passion for water is a lifelong story about learning and experiencing the science and mathematics of fluids in motion, balance and force interactions, water density, homeostasis and temperature regulation, and aquatic life.

Overcoming Fear and Jumping

My family's summer visits to the nice cool Wakulla Springs State Park in northern Florida was a welcome change from the Florida summer heat. As a state park and one of the largest and deepest freshwater springs in the world, the beautiful springs of crystal clear, aqua-colored waters are such that you can see the sandy bottom of the pools. It is home for abundant wildlife including alligators, turtles, manatees, deer, and birds, which you can see as you hike or from the jungle boat tour. You also can swim in the waters of the springs and jump from two ledges, now concrete platforms, of different heights. Local children would delight in climbing onto and jumping off them. The higher one is about five meters high.

My middle son, Tal, really wanted to jump from the higher ledge, but he was afraid. He would climb onto this ledge, look over its edge to the water below, and then climb back down. One day while he was standing at the edge, one of his older brother's friends suddenly and violently pushed him. Tal dropped into the spring water. Fun! No more fear! From then on, it was easy to jump and free-fall. If his brother's friend had not pushed him, and though he wanted to, he might never have jumped. Like the other stories in this chapter, this example of everyday science and mathematics is multi-dimensional: the biology of the fear emotion and role of hormones on body systems and response of body systems; height, motion, and free fall physics; aquatic biology; properties of water; and environmental appreciation.

They Bite – Ouch and Itch!

This story is about the everyday science and mathematics of the human body's defense mechanisms - immunological response, which for some people could have an allergic reaction, with resulting neuromuscular interactions and motion. It is a biology story about life cycles, insect habitats and ecological relationships, and environmental awareness. It is a weather and mathematics story about climate, precipitation and depth of accumulated water. It is a story of human inquiry entailing oral communication of knowledge, direct observation, and use of inductive reasoning.

When we lived in the Florida Panhandle, we continued a favorite family activity – going to the seashore on the weekends. If we were still on the beach at sunset and the wind was not blowing, we would find that when we walked back to the car, we were covered with little, itchy bumps from no-see-um encounters. Ouch! We quickly learned on windless days to get back to the car before sunset.

Neither did we know about another insect with a painful bite. Fire ants that left a horrible welt from their poison after biting through the skin! Summer days, summer rains. The fire ants would accumulate and swim in water pools in depressions, some of them located at the base of trees. These pools could be up to four feet deep. The locals knew about them; we did not. The local children knew where the water would pool after these torrential rains, and they would jump into the pools to play and cool off. Since my sons loved being in the water, they would follow. It was fun until they realized they had been bitten by fire ants and had a number of welts, and the bites were extremely itchy. The boys quickly learned not to put their heads under water, because being bit on the body was not as painful as being bit on the head. We were fortunate that the boys did not have an allergic reaction to the poisons from these insects, like others might have.

Questions Set 6.2:

1. What interested you during the elementary school years? What were your past-times and hobbies during non-school hours?
2. Form pairs and share your memories. Pick one non-school activity and discuss the science and mathematics that is related to these interests and activities.
3. Draw a picture depicting one non-school activity from this time in your life, being sure to visually depict ways that science and mathematics were involved.

EVERYDAY SCIENCE AND MATHEMATICS DURING FORMAL SCHOOLING – SECONDARY

Physical and emotional health, safety, and savvy consumerism, continue to be a focus for learning during the secondary school years. In these years life becomes more complex because we are members of many communities simultaneously –

family, school, friends, community-based social groups, and perhaps church organizations and work worlds. We need to make healthy wise choices and financially sound decisions, as informed citizens who can read and understand research, engage in argumentation (Erduran & Jimenez-Aleixandre, 2008), and sift through claims made by family, friends, teachers, and the media.

I remember when my youngest son Ido was in middle school, he became a three-point basketball shooting star. Though athletic for his size, being overweight at the time he was not quick enough to run around the players on the other team, especially the guards. His only option as a player on a Parks and Recreation youth league team was to become a shooting guard and star. He practiced every day with the backyard hoop and his friends. Ido made the best choice he could to take advantage of his physical condition at that time.

Science and Mathematics in Everyday Decisions of Teens

During the adolescent years, youth learn to drive cars, an activity involving extensive science and mathematics knowledge; such as distance estimation, distance and time relationships in the context of speed of vehicles, and possibly the effects of drug use on reaction times and ability to gauge distances.

The media bombard the youth with media messages to look, dress, move, react, and interact in certain ways, regardless whether a product or a style will enhance their natural beauty and complexion, or not. They face questions: Do I dress in the current fashion of this social clique or that one? Do I wear makeup or not? If I walk down this street at night or in this hallway, will I be unharmed? Will he or she use birth control, and will it work? Is my money better spent in eating at this restaurant, on that cell phone plan because of its start-up costs and conditions, on that movie, etc.?

Teens must be informed about factors that affect their health and well-being, like smoking and drug use (prescribed and recreational), food and diet choices, constantly loud sounds and music through earphones and headsets, decisions related to sexual activity, allergic reactions, and costs (environmental and human) to create and bring products to local and virtual store fronts.

Teens need to know the process of making sound financial decisions and be able to budget their earnings from part- or full-time work.

Geometry, Vectors and Budgeting—Physics of Play at Game Consoles

When our sons were growing up, we would give them a set amount of pocket money to spend on entertainment. We would give them $20 entertainment money, and when the $20 was gone, the entertainment was over. Going to the arcades was a regular weekend event during their middle and high school years in Bellingham, Washington. When we went to Las Vegas, Nevada, they as children could not gamble so they spent their days at the arcade games. Each son had a different favorite game at the arcade park, depending on the length of time they could play for the price of one game.

Tal's favorite cost 50 cents per game and was a certain genre of digital games that involved up to three, two-dimensional, hand-drawn characters fighting against another player's characters. The person with the last character alive was the winner. People wanting to play would put their quarters on the arcade game to show they wanted to play against you. Tal once beat 24 other people in a row (each game lasting about 1.5 minutes) – 36 minutes of game play on fifty cents. Only because he was hungry and wanted to eat, did he give up his spot to someone else. Fifty cents could last a half hour or more before he would lose and have to give up his spot at the game. Playing this game stretched his money so he could entertain himself all day long. He liked the complexity and the violence of this genre of games. At the time he did not make the connection between playing these digital games that have animation in them and an interest in animation. The first time he remembers being interested in animation was at age seven, watching the television program, The Simpsons. Now, he sees the connection between these early experiences –the cool graphics of the TV show and mortal combat pictures set to a faster frame rate in the game, and now he has a desire to work in the profession of animation after completing studies in illustration, cartoon drawing, and animation.

Ido spent his money in a totally different way. His favorite arcade park game was a basketball shooting game that cost four quarters, in which if you did well, you walked away with a prize. In this game if you made a certain number of shots, you would receive a small basketball as the prize. He was so good at the game that he collected about a hundred of these small balls. Though he does not live at home anymore, they are still in his room. Maybe his game preference was a seed for his later decision to study and work in the business field.

The above examples of everyday science and mathematics have connections to the mathematics and economics of travel, the biomechanics and mathematics of sport and leisure activity, the influence of probability in game play, the importance of quick computation, the physical sciences of transportation, the science-technology-society triangle in the context of electricity and electronics, and the biology of communication. The stories also make the point that adulthood decisions about job and career, hobbies and leisure time interests may be linked to experiences when one was a baby, young child, and adolescent. Who needs science and mathematics? Each of us needs science and mathematics in our everyday lives. We need to begin understanding that science and mathematics knowledge can act as tools for engaging in and making sense of all life experiences, and that we need these tools from an early age in order to be educated and informed individuals, consumers and 21st century global citizens.

Questions Set 6.3:

1. What interested you when you attended secondary (middle and high) school? What media messages or social pressures related to your areas of interest did you encounter? How did the media messages or social pressures affect the choices you made?
2. Form pairs and share your memories.

3. With your partner, brainstorm examples of media messages and research claims that secondary youth today might encounter. Where are the science and mathematics connections in these messages and claims?

EVERYDAY SCIENCE AND MATHEMATICS – AN ULTIMATE CHALLENGE FOR HUMAN EXISTENCE, A STORY OF CANCER

I am a scientist, science educator, professional, mother, wife, friend and a patient who has lived with and died from ovarian cancer. At age 56, I was forced to retire from my profession because I could not continue to teach, though I wish I could. Five and one half years ago I listened to the words, "ovarian cancer." As a cognizing emotional being, hearing these words was a shock. Like a mouse whose life becomes owned by a researcher, instantaneously, I became a cancer patient. My reaction then had many dimensions because I am not one-dimensional. I am (we are) not only a cognizing being; I am (we are) an emotional being too. Retiring at age 56 because I cannot continue to work was tough, because when I think about retirement, I think of it as a time to enjoy the fruits and successes of work and life. It is a time to re-view one's life. Accompanying the phrase and diagnosis, ovarian cancer, I was also told that I would not have the days to enjoy these fruits. Instead, decisions became forced. I retired and live with a journey of immense physical pain with little pleasure. For me, retirement at 56 was a detriment to my students, my family and myself. I cannot pursue my passions any more. I would read "at 65 (the typical age for thinking about pension) …", and instead think, "What 65 years of age? I am 56 years old!"

As a scientist, the diagnosis was a shock for me, "We do not have a solution!" Individuals have been working for decades investigating cancer diseases and conducting research and clinical studies in search of causes and mechanisms, the aim being to discover solutions to stop its destruction. Despite all the research and clinical studies we are still faced with something so devastating. We have advanced so much in our science and mathematics knowledge, yet how do we comprehend terminal illnesses like cancer? We are more familiar with illness that goes away, and this one does not. We know so much, and yet it is not enough. Although I am an informed person, the knowledge is not easily available nor is it easily comprehended, so it is hard to sift through what is known. Neither is there an organized system to inform patients. My husband received 27 clinical studies of ovarian cancer. I read studies in which molecular gene therapy - nanotechnology to package ribonucleic acids into cancer cells to destroy them from the inside - was being investigated in the context of the treatment of cancer (Butler & Senior, 2007). Our idea was to try to approach the right clinical study in which to participate, but how does one sift through the knowledge base to make a choice? We are far away from having this knowledge as tools so individuals can make appropriate choices.

After five and a half years of fighting the cancer, can I say that the mathematics and science research and medical communities have failed me (and others who have lived with and died from cancer)? I do not know. How can we do early detection when no test exists to detect a problem? If I had known decades ago what I know now aboout ovarian cancer and its risk factors, because of my high risk status, I would have had a total hysterectomy, and my travel through life might have turned out differently. Choices and decisions for individuals in high-risk situations are different than those for individuals not in high-risk situations. In my case the battle with an aggressive form of ovarian cancer has been a dynamic process, since the cancer changed over time. Not only did the cancer metastasize, it mutated so chemotherapy had no effect. My body came to not recognize the cancer hidden in and taking over its cells. If my body had recognized the cancer cells as foreign, then the immunological system would have been mobilized.

Questions Set 6.4:

1. What do you think is the ultimate challenge, and why?
2. Are the schooling systems preparing children and youth with the tools and skills to face, address and resolve this ultimate challenge? How? If not, what needs to be done differently?
3. After reflecting on these two questions, get together in small groups and share your responses.

IN THE END WHAT REALLY MATTERS?

A major reason for writing this book was the impact of cancer on my life. I am very impulsive and jumpy, and I have always thought that it is good to be emotional.

> Without exception, men and women of all ages, of all cultures, of all levels of education, and of all walks of economic life have emotions, are mindful of the emotions of others, cultivate pastimes that manipulate their emotions and govern their lives in no small part by the pursuit of one's emotion, happiness, and the avoidance of unpleasant emotions. (Damasio, 2000, p. 35)

Battling with and dying from cancer has changed me. The journey has brought my own mortality into perspective, and I have come to understand differently the role of emotion, especially the experience of pain. I feel and think that now I am becoming more human. I realize what counts and matters, and is most important in life. My strongest interest now is the undeniable connection of cognition and emotion, a relationship, which still confuses me, but I know is critical for learning (and living a passionate and fulfilled life).

When I began writing this book, I was intrigued by the concept of emotional intelligence and ways that emotions help us to make sense of our worlds and reach best conclusions. As I continued to write and as my travel through life became a fight against cancer, I wanted to understand the nature of the connection between cognition and emotion. More than ever, now (the last few days of my life), and though complete understanding of the connection still eludes me, I firmly believe that it is good to recognize emotions and maximize the benefit from the existence of interconnectedness of emotion and cognition, all of which happen in the brain.

When *Homo sapiens* learns, whether in a school classroom or other classrooms of life, feelings and emotions are part of the learning experience. Emotions – like apathy, boredom, frustration, insecurity, embarrassment, confidence, happiness, pride, curiosity, and excitement - exist in all classrooms of learning. When students and teacher care about learning, the classroom is full of passion. Because emotion is an important part of learning and is totally interconnected with cognition, *Homo sapiens* must pay attention to it.

Let us revisit an idea, which I developed in previous chapters. Teachers in school classrooms, and thus indirectly society, try to educate children and youth. Many students feel unsuccessful in and disconnected from school classroom environments. Schools are not meeting the demands for recognition by the social groups and cliques represented in the student population (like snowboarders, skaters, surfers, nerds, social outcasts, in-group). When this desire for recognition as a group with its own pleasures goes unmet, connecting these students and group interests to school lessons is problematic, as the students do not perceive school learning as meaningful. They are not valuing the schooling experience, and so they choose not to participate.

A student needs to feel that she has an asset or strength to offer and contribute in order to participate in a conversation of learning. Teachers need to recognize the assets and strengths – the pluses – that each student brings to the classroom. Only then will students feel recognized and valued, and come to and sit at the table of school learning. As an example, a student works in the construction industry during off-school hours. Classmates view her as having expertise in this field. When she talks about her work in construction, her eyes are lit with excitement and her classmates listen attentively. What happens when this student enters the school classroom? Perhaps the student is intimidated by book terminology in the sciences and mathematics, and lectures because they do not make sense to her. She may think that science and mathematics knowledge are merely algorithmic in nature, instead of particular understandings. She may make choices, based on these algorithmic understandings. She may not necessarily know that her understandings are tools of science and mathematics in everyday life, and that her knowledge and expertise are assets, which she can contribute to a learning conversation. She knows that she feels intimidated and unsuccessful. Thus, she chooses not to participate in school learning. Her expertise remains hidden from and not known by schoolteachers. Her willingness to show and help others goes unrecognized.

What is an alternative? A teacher discovers the student as a person. A teacher recognizes the student's strengths and expertise, and uses these strengths and expertise so students see meaningfulness and connectedness of school learning to living life. Through this choice the teacher helps students to participate in school learning. A teacher cannot take a student who feels that she knows nothing or has nothing to contribute, and get her to participate in school learning.

On a personal level, like the student in a school classroom, I have wanted to show and help others. I have wanted to use my strengths and expertise to add something to the science and mathematics education conversation. Like many of my colleagues, I have focused on my career and profession. I am not saying that this choice was the wrong choice for me. No - it was the right choice for that time in my life. Over the years though, I have observed increasing numbers of faculty disgusted and disappointed by the professoriate pathway. Somewhere in this journey of focusing on career and profession, I believe that we (and I) lose something of our humanity and our spirit.

Orloff (2005) and Damasio (2000) have written that there is much more to life than greets our senses and cognition. That something involves the critical importance of our human relationships and the integration of something spiritual in one's life. While thinking about this chapter, I was reading Judith Orloff's *Positive Energy* (2005), and I really like the ideas that she shares about moving from negative energies into positive energies. What matters is focusing on and cultivating positive energy through attention to and time with friends and family. After five and one half years of battling cancer, I look less in directions that I used to look. I look more toward the need and importance of positive emotions; I choose to avoid people exuding negative energy (Orloff, 2005). I do not want to be around people angry at little nit-picky things and put their energy into negative aspects of living.

I remember the stories of friends who have made choices to decisively focus on and cultivate positive energies. Katherine Wieseman who resigned from a tenured professor position in teacher education, and as part of her new life journey went to South Africa for a month. She spoke of how the South Africans she met had opened their homes to her, sharing their strong belief of being in a community. Mutindi mumbua ndunda, another colleague in science education, shared that in her return visit to the simple village life of Kenya, life was so pleasant. The villagers truly lived in community with each other; they lived their strong value of community. A colleague at my California State University campus, Irene Osisioma, returns yearly to Nigeria to recharge her batteries to deal with the pressures of living and working in academia the USA.

And I have learned that above all, "love is the most positive energy we have" (Orloff, 2005, p. 157) (Figure 6.2).

Figure 6.2. Above all...

Question Set 6.5:

1. What is your answer to the question: in the end, what really matters to you to learn science, learn math, learn to teach science and math, *Homo sapiens*?

NOTES

[3] Katherine Wieseman was with Hedy during the last week of Hedy's life. During the early days of this week when Hedy was able, Katherine gathered information to form a framework of Hedy's ideas for chapter 6. Meanwhile, Penny Gilmer was editing the initial chapters so Katherine and Hedy's son, Tal Moscovici, could ask for clarification of confusing aspects, to help Katherine's work with Hedy. Expanding on Hedy's ideas and through interviewing her sons, Danny, Tal and Ido during this and the week after Hedy's death, Katherine was able to write this chapter to complete the book and ready it and the earlier five chapters for further editing by Penny and Katherine.

BIBLIOGRAPHY

AAAS Project 2061. (1998). *Guide Book to Examine School Curricula: The Project 2061 Curriculum-analysis Procedure.*

AAAS Project 2061. (2002). *Middle Grades Science Textbooks: A Benchmarks-based Evaluation.* Retrieved from http://www.project2061.org/publications/textbook/mgsci/report/crit-used.htm#3

AAAS Project 2061. (2012). *Guide Book to Examine School Curricula: The Project 2061 Curriculum-analysis Procedure.* Retrieved from http://www.project2061.org/publications/articles/enc/enctims.htm

Aerts, D., Apostel, L., De Moor, B., Hellemans, S., Maex, E., Van Belle, H., et al. (2007). *World Views: From Fragmentation to Integration.* Retrieved from http://www.vub.ac.be/CLEA/pub/books/worldviews.pdf

American Institutes of Research. (2007). *Successful California Schools in the Context of Educational Adequacy.* Retrieved from http://irepp.stanford.edu/documents/GDF/STUDIES/17-AIR-Successful-Schools/17-Successful-California-Schools(3-07).pdf

Amrein-Beardsley, A. (2008). Methodological concerns about the education value-added assessment system. *Educational Researcher, 37*(2), 65–75.

Anyon, J. (1980). Social class and the hidden curriculum of work. *Journal of Education, 162*(1), 67–92.

Anyon, J. (1997). *Ghetto Schooling: A Political Economy of Urban Educational Reform.* New York: Teachers College Press.

Aronowitz, S., & Giroux, H. A. (1993). *Education Still under Siege* (2nd ed.). Westport, CT: Bergin & Garvey.

Arsenie, D., & Dan, O. (2009). *Jocurile Copilariei, Generatie cu Generatie.* [tr: Games of childhood, generation after generation]. Retrieved from http://www.evz.ro/detalii/stiri/jocurile-copilariei-generatie-cu-generatie-875586.html

Ashkanasy, N. M., Trevor-Roberts, E., & Earnshaw, L. (2001). *The Anglo Cluster: Legacy of the British Empire.* Retrieved from http://espace.library.uq.edu.au/eserv.php?pid=UQ:13565&dsID=Ashkanasy_Trevor-Woods_Earnshaw_Final_2001.pdf [Later published in Journal of *World Business* (2002), *37*(1): 28–39].

Bauersfeld. (1988). Interaction, construction, and knowledge: Alternative perspectives for mathematics education. In T. Cooney & D. Grouws (Eds.), *Effective Mathematics Teaching* (pp. 27–46). Reston, VA: National Council of Teachers of Mathematics and Lawrence Erlbaum Associates.

Bausmith, J. M., & Barry, C. (2011). Revisiting professional learning communities to increase college readiness: The importance of pedagogical content knowledge. *Educational Researcher, 40*(4), 175–178.

Big Dog and Little Dog. (2010, revised). Leadership style survey. Retrieved from http://www.nwlink.com/~donclark/leader/survstyl.html

Bloom, B. S., Hastings, J. T., & Madaus, G. F. (Eds.). (1971). *Handbook on Formative and Summative Evaluation of Student Learning.* New York: McGraw-Hill Book Company.

Boeree, C. G. (1997). *Alfred Adler.* Retrieved from http://borderlinepersonality.ca/alfredadler.htm

Boeree, C. G. (2009a). *Neurotransmitters.* Retrieved from http://webspace.ship.edu/cgboer/genpsyneurotransmitters.html

Boeree, C. G. (2009b). *Personality Theory: A Biosocial Approach.* Retrieved from http://webspace.ship.edu/cgboer/ptpsychdis.html

BrainU. (2011). *Teacher Guide: Mirroring Emotions.* Retrieved from http://brainu.org/

Bransford, J. D., Brown, A. L., & Cocking, R. R. (Eds.). (2000). *How People Learn: Brain, Mind, Experience, and School.* Washington, DC: National Academy Press.

Bransford, J. D., & Donovan, M. S. (2005). Scientific inquiry and How People Learn. In M. S. Donovan & J. D. Bransford (Eds.), *How Students Learn: History, Mathematics, and Science in the Classroom* (pp. 397–419). Washington, DC: National Academies Press.

Brigido, M., Bermejo, M. L., Conde, M. C, & Mellado, V. (2010). The emotions in teaching and learning nature sciences and physics/chemistry in pre-service primary teachers. *US-China Education Review, 7*(12), 25–32.

Butler, M. J. R., & Senior, C. (2007). Toward an organizational cognitive neuroscience. *Annals of the New York Academy of Sciences, 1118*, 1–17. Retrieved from http://www.ncbi.nlm.nih.gov/pmc/articles/PMC2837361/

Byrnes, J. P. (2008). Math skills. In Jossey-Bass (Ed.), *The Jossey-Bass Reader on the Brain and Learning* (pp. 301–327). San Francisco: John Wiley & Sons, Inc.

California Department of Education. (1998). *Science Content Standards for California Public Schools: Kindergarten through Grade Twelve.* Sacramento, CA: Author.

Carroll, C., & Mumme, J. (2011). *Developing MKT: Tasks that Support Teachers' Specialized Content Knowledge.* WestEd. Retrieved from http://www.teachersdg.org/2011Seminar%20Docs/Carroll%20&%20Mumme%20Tasks%20for%20SCK%202011.pdf

Cherry, K. (2010). *Background and Key Concepts of Piaget's Theory.* Retrieved from http://psychology.about.com/od/piagetstheory/a/keyconcepts.htm

Chiu, M. H. (2009). International Committee Report. *E-NARST News, 52*(2), 14.

Cobern, W. W. (1991). *World View Theory and Science Education Research*, NARST Monograph No. 3. Manhattan, KS: National Association for Research in Science Teaching.

Cobern, W. W. (1993). Contextual constructivism: The impact of culture on the learning and teaching of science. In K. Tobin (Ed.), *The Practice of Constructivism in Science Education* (pp. 51–69). Hillsdale, NJ: Lawrence-Erlbaum.

Cobern, W. W. (1994). *Worldview Theory and Conceptual Change in Science Education.* Retrieved from http://www.wmich.edu/slcsp/SLCSP124/SLCSP-124.pdf

Cox, C. A., & Carpenter, J. R. (1989). Improving attitudes toward teaching science and reducing science anxiety through increasing confidence in science ability in inservice elementary school teachers. *Journal of Elementary Science Education, 1*(8), 14–34.

Csikszentmihalyi, M. (1990). *Flow: The Psychology of Optimal Experience.* New York: Harper & Row, Publishers.

Cunningham, W. G., & Cordeiro, P. A. (2006). *Educational Leadership: A Problem-based Approach* (3rd ed.). Boston: Pearson Education, Inc.

Dalgleish, T. (2004). The emotional brain. *Nature Reviews Neuroscience, 5*, 583–589.

Damasio, A. (2000). *The Feeling of What Happens – Body, Emotion and the Making of Consciousness.* London: Vintage.

Daniels, H., & Bizar, M. (2005). *Teaching the Best Practice Way: Methods that Matter, K-12.* Portland, ME: Stenhouse Publishers.

De Martino, B., Kumaran, D., Seymour, B., & Dolan, R. J. (2006). Frames, biases, and rational decision-making in the human brain. *Science, 313*, 684–687.

Donovan, M. S. & Bransford, J. D. (Eds.). (2005a). *How Students Learn: Science in the Classroom.* Washington, DC: The National Academies Press. Retrieved from http://www.nap.edu/catalog.php?record_id=11102

Donovan, M. S. & Bransford, J. D (Eds.). (2005b). *How Students Learn: Mathematics in the Classroom.* Washington, DC: The National Academies Press. Retrieved from http://www.nap.edu/catalog.php?record_id=11101#toc

Donovan, M. S., & Bransford, J. D. (2005c). Introduction. In M. S. Donovan & J. D. Bransford (Eds.), *How Students Learn: History, Mathematics, and Science in the Classroom* (pp. 1–28). Washington, DC: National Academies Press.

Einstein, A. (2003). Physics and reality. *Daedalus, 132*(4), 22–25. Retrieved from http://www.mitpressjournals.org/doi/abs/10.1162/001152603771338742

Ekman, P. (1999). Basic emotions. In T. Dalgleish & M. Power (Eds.), *Handbook of Cognition and Emotion* (pp. 45–60). Sussex, U.K.: John Wiley & Sons, Ltd. Retrieved from http://www.paulekman.com/wp-content/uploads/2009/02/Basic-Emotions.pdf

Enfield, N. J. (2010). Language evolution: Without social context? *Science, 329*(5999), 1600–1601.

English, F. W. (2008). *The Art of Educational Leadership: Balancing Performance and Accountability.* Thousand Oaks, CA: Sage publications, Inc.

Erduran, S. & Jimenez-Aleixandre, M. P. (Eds.). (2008). *Argumentation in Science Education: Perspectives from Classroom-based Research.* Dordrecht, The Netherlands: Springer.

Fields, H. L. (2007). *Pain Perception–The Dana Guide.* Retrieved from http://www.dana.org/news/brainhealth/detail.aspx?id=10072

Fisher, K. W., Goswami, U., Geake, J., & Task Force on the Future of Educational Neuroscience. (2010). The future of educational neuroscience. *Mind, Brain, and Education, 4*(2), 68–80.

Fisher, K. W., Wang, L., Kennedy, B., & Cheng, C-L. (1998). Culture and biology in emotional development. *New Directions for Child Development, 81,* 21–43.

Foucault, M. (1979). *Discipline and Punish: The Birth of the Prison.* New York: Vintage Books.

Foucault, M. (1980). *Power/knowledge: Selected Interviews & Other Writings 1972–1977.* New York: Pantheon Books.

Freire, P. (1990). *Pedagogy of the Oppressed.* New York: Continuum.

Freire, P. (1998). *Teachers as Cultural Workers: Letters to Those Who Dare Teach.* Boulder, CO: Westview Press.

Fridja, N. H. (2008). The psychologist's point of view. In M. Lewis, J. M. Haviland-Jones, & L. F. Barrett (Eds.), *Handbook of Emotions* (3rd ed., pp. 68–87). New York: The Guilford Press.

Friesen, N. (2011). The lecture as transmedial pedagogical form: A historical analysis. *Educational Researcher, 40*(3), 95–102.

Fuson, K. C., Kalchman, M., & Bransford, J. D. (2005). Mathematical understanding: An introduction. In M. S. Donovan & J. D. Bransford (Eds.), *How Students Learn: History, Mathematics, and Science in the Classroom* (pp. 217–256). Washington, DC: National Academies Press.

Gadino, B. (2006). *There are No Basic Emotions.* Retrieved from http://www.csun.edu/~gk45683/P691%20Gadino%20Presentation.pdf

Gamoran, A., Anderson, C. W., Quiroz, P. A., Secada, W. G., Williams, T., & Ashmann, S. (2003). *Transforming Teaching in Math and Science: How Schools and Districts can Support Change.* New York: Teachers College Press.

Gardner, H. (1983). *Frames of Mind: The Theory of Multiple Intelligences.* New York: Basic Books.

Gardner, H. (1991). *The Unschooled Mind: How Children Think and How Schools should Teach.* New York: Basic Books.

Garmston, R. J. (2000a). Harmonious duos. *Journal of Staff Development, 21*(2), 65–67. Retrieved from http://www.learningforward.org/news/jsd/garmston212.cfm

Garmston, R. J. (2000b). Ouch! These six slips can bruise and strain a presentation. *Journal of Staff Development, 21*(4), 76–77. Retrieved from http://www.learningforward.org/news/jsd/garmston214.cfm

Garmston, R. J., & Wellman, B. M. (1999). *The Adaptive School: A Sourcebook for Developing Collaborative Groups.* Norwood, MA: Christopher-Gordon Publishers, Inc.

Genes to Cognition Online. (2011) *Amygdala.* Retrieved from http://www.g2conline.org/2104

Gergen, K. J. (1995). Social construction and the educational process. In L. P. Steffe & J. Gale (Eds.), *Constructivism in Education* (pp. 17–39). Hillsdale, NJ: Lawrence Erlbaum.

Gess-Newsome, J. & Lederman, N. G. (Eds.). (1999). *Examining Pedagogical Content Knowledge: The Construct and Its Implications for Science Education.* Dordrecht, The Netherlands: Kluwer Academic Publishers.

Gilbert, D. (2007). Science and happiness: Interview with Daniel Gilbert. In L. Margulis & E. Punset (Eds.), *Mind, Life and Universe: Conversations with Great Scientists of our Time* (pp. 58–67). White River Junction, VT: Chelsea Green Publishing Book.

Giroux, H. A., & Simon, R. (1989). Popular culture and critical pedagogy: Everyday life as a basis for curriculum knowledge. In H. A. Giroux & P. L. McLaren (Eds.), *Critical Pedagogy, the State and Cultural Struggle* (pp. 236–252). New York: State University of New York Press.

Glanz, J. (2002). *Finding Your Leadership Style: A Guide for Educators.* Alexandria, VA: Association for Supervision and Curriculum Development (ASCD).

Glanz, J. (2003). *Leading with Soul and Conviction: Essential Qualities and Virtues for Effective Leadership.* Retrieved from http://www.q3.ca/articles/archives/articles/02-01-2006/Leading_with_Soul_and_Conviction.pdf

Glanz, J. (2011). *What Every Principal Should Know about Collaborative Leadership.* Retrieved from http://books.google.com/books?hl=en&lr=&id=d6fDaf3oWS0C&oi=fnd&pg=PR8&dq=Glanz+and+leadership+survey&ots=0NBbaKLG3L&sig=MupJI97crJZwTr6NGrDF9QiI-yw#v=onepage&q=Glanz%20and%20leadership%20survey&f=false

Glanz, J. (2012). *Finding Your Leadership Style: A Guide for Educators. Introduction.* Retrieved from http://www.ascd.org/publications/books/102115/chapters/Introduction.aspx

Glasersfeld, E. (1988). The reluctance to change a way of thinking. *Irish Journal of Psychology, 9*(1), 83–90.

Glasersfeld, E. (1989). Abstraction, representation, and reflection. In L. P. Steffe (Ed.), *Epistemological Foundations of Mathematical Experience* (pp. 45–67). Dordrecht, The Netherlands: Springer.

Glasersfeld, E. (1991a). Answers to the NARST meeting in Atlanta and the AAAS meeting in Washington, DC questions. Draft.

Glasersfeld, E. (Ed.). (1991b). *Radical Constructivism in Mathematics Education.* Dordrecht, the Netherlands: Kluwer Academic Publishers.

Glasersfeld, E., & Cobb, P. (1983). *Knowledge as Environmental Fit.* Retrieved from http://www.vonglasersfeld.com/084

Glickman, C. D. (2002). *Leadership for Learning: How to Help Teachers Succeed.* Alexandria, VA: Association for Supervision and Curriculum Development (ASCD).

Goleman, D. (1995). *Emotional Intelligence: Why It Can Matter More Than IQ.* New York: Bantam Books.

Grewal, D., & Salovey, P. (2005). Feeling smart: The science of emotional intelligence. *American Scientist, 93*(4), 330–339.

Grundy, S. (1987). *Curriculum: Product or Praxis?* Philadelphia: The Falmer Press.

Hall, G. E., & Hord, S. M. (2006). *Implementing Change: Patterns, Principles, and Potholes* (2nd ed.). Boston: Pearson Education Inc.

Helms, J. E., & Barone, C. P. (2008). Physiology and treatment of pain. *Critical Care Nurse, 28*(6), 38–50. Retrieved from http://www.aacn.org/WD/CETests/Media/C0863.pdf

Herreid, C. F. (2001). The maiden and the witch: The crippling undergraduate experience. *Journal of College Science Teaching, 36*(2), 87–88.

Heschl, A. (2002). *The Intelligent Genome: On the Origin of the Human Mind by Mutation and Selection.* New York: Springer.

Holton, G. (1994). The antiscience problem. *Skeptical Inquirer, 18*, 264–265.

Hopley, L., & van Schalkwyk, J. (2006). *Pain Physiology.* Retrieved from http://www.anaesthetist.com/icu/pain/Findex.htm#pain3.htm

Huber, S. G. (2004). School leadership and leadership development: Adjusting leadership theories and development programs to values and the core purpose of school. *Journal of Educational Administration, 42*(6), 669–684.

Hughes, L. (2012). *Dreams.* Retrieved from http://www.poemhunter.com/poem/dreams-2/

Humintell. (2011). *The Seven Basic Emotions: Do You Know Them?* Retrieved from http://www.humintell.com/2010/06/the-seven-basic-emotions-do-you-know-them/

Immordino-Yang, M. H., & Damasio, A. (2008). We feel, therefore we learn: The relevance of affective and social neuroscience to education. In Jossey-Bass (Ed.), *The Jossey-Bass Reader on the Brain and Learning* (pp. 183–198). San Francisco: John Wiley & Sons, Inc.

Isen, A. M. (2008). Some ways in which positive affect influences decision making and problem solving. In M. Lewis, J. M. Haviland-Jones, & Barrett, L. F. (Eds.), *Handbook of Emotions* (3rd ed., pp. 548–573). New York: The Guilford Press.

Izard, C. E. (1992). Basic emotions, relations among emotions, and emotion-cognition relations. *Psychological Review, 99*(3), 561–565. Retrieved from http://dionysus.psych.wisc.edu/Lit/Articles/IzardC1992a.pdf

Jackson, R. R. (2009). *Never Work Harder Than Your Students & Other Principles of Great Teaching.* Alexandria, VA: ASCD.

Jacobs, H. H. (Ed.). (2010). *Curriculum 21: Essential Education for a Changing World.* Alexandria, VA: Association for Supervision and Curriculum Development (ASCD).

Jandt, F. E. (2007). *An Introduction to Intercultural Communication: Identities in a Global Community* (5th ed.). Thousand Oaks, CA: Sage Publications.

Joubert, J. (1842). *Pensées.* Retrieved from http://www.quotegarden.com/teachers.html

Kaser, J., Mundry, S., Stiles, K. E., & Loucks-Horsley, S. (2006). *Leading Every Day: 124 Actions for Effective Leadership* (2nd ed.). Thousand Oaks, CA: Corwin Press, A Sage Publication Company.

Kearney, M. (1975). World view theory and study. *Annual Review of Anthropology, 4,* 247–270.

Kearney, M. (1984). *World View.* Novato, CA: Chandler & Sharp Publishers, Inc.

Keyser, J. O. (1993). The Science Learning Center at Maryland's Montgomery College. *Journal of College Science Teaching, 23*(1), 25–28.

King, M. W. (2011). *Table of Neurotransmitters.* Retrieved from http://themedicalbiochemistrypage.org/nerves.html

Kitonga, N. (2010). *Postcolonial Construction of Self: Two Immigrant Secondary Science Teachers from Nigeria and Kenya Explore the Role of Cultural and Indigenous Beliefs in their Teaching.* Unpublished Doctoral Dissertation, Chapman University, Orange County, California.

Kohls, R. (1990, April). Modèles de comparaison des cultures (Models for Contrasting and Comparing Cultures). *Intercultures, 9.* [citation from, Author unknown.] (2011, March 2). *Cross Cultural Glossary.* Retrieved from http://www.akteos.com/interculturel/outils-services/cross-cultural-glossary/

Kozma. (2005). National policies that connect ICT-based education reform to economic and social development. *International Journal on Humans in ICT Environments, 1*(2), 117–156. Retrieved from https://jyx.jyu.fi/dspace/handle/123456789/20179

Lampert, M. (1986). Knowing, doing, and teaching multiplication. *Cognition and Instruction, 3*(4), 305–342. [for more information, see web site of Magdalene Lampert – publications at http://www-personal.umich.edu/~mlampert/Publications.htm]

Larsen, J. T., Berntson, G. G., Poehlmann, K. M., Ito, T. A., & Cacciopo, J. T. (2008). The psychophysiology of emotion. In M. Lewis, J. M. Haviland-Jones, & L. F. Barrett (Eds.), *Handbook of Emotions* (3rd ed., pp. 180–195). New York: The Guilford Press.

LeDoux, J. E. (1987). The neurobiology of emotions. In J. E. LeDoux & W. Hirst (Eds.), *Mind and Brain: Dialogues in Cognitive Neuroscience* (pp. 301–354). New York: Cambridge University Press.

LeDoux, J. (1996). *The Emotional Brain.* New York: Simon & Schuster.

LeDoux, J. E., & Hirst, W. (1987). *Mind and Brain: Dialogues in Cognitive Neuroscience.* New York: Cambridge University Press.

Lemke, J. L. (1989). The language of science teaching. In C. Emihovich (Ed.), *Locating Learning: Ethnographic Perspectives on Classroom Research* (pp. 216–239). Norwood, NJ: Ablex Publishing Corporation.

Lemke, J. L. (1990). *Talking Science: Language, Learning, and Values.* Norwood, NJ: Ablex Publishing Company.

Lemke, J. L. (1992, May/June). Personal narrative & academic discourse: Tools for making meaning. *Liberal Education, 78*(3), 28–33.

Lemke, J. L. (1998). Multiplying meaning: Visual and verbal semiotics in scientific text. In J. R. Martin & R. Veel (Eds.), *Reading Science: Critical and Functional Perspectives on Discourses of Science* (pp. 87–113). New York: Routledge.

Loucks-Horsley, S., Love, N., Stiles, K. E., Mundry, S., & Hewson, P. W. (2003). *Designing Professional Development for Teachers of Science and Mathematics* (3rd ed.). Thousand Oaks, CA: Corwin Press.

Love, N., Stiles, N. E., Mundry, S., & DiRanna, K. (2008). *The Data Coach's Guide to Improving Learning for All Students: Unleashing the Power of Collaborative Inquiry.* Thousands Oaks, CA: Corwin Press, A SAGE Company.

Ma, L. (1999). *Knowing and Teaching Elementary Mathematics: Teachers' Understanding of Fundamental Mathematics in China and the United States*. Mahwah, NJ: Lawrence Erlbaum Associates, Publishers.

Ma, L. (2001). *Arithmetic in American Mathematics Education: An Abandoned Arena?* Retrieved from http://www.cbmsweb.org/nationalSummit/Plenary_Speakers/ma.htm

Mallow, J. V. (1978). A prescription for science anxiety. *Science, 17*(4), 330–331.

Mallow, J. V. (1981). New cures for science anxiety. *Science, 20*(4), 389–391.

Mallow, J. V. (1986). *Science Anxiety: Fear of Science and How to Overcome It*. Clearwater, FL: H & H Publishing Co., Inc.

Matthews, B. (2004). Promoting emotional literacy, equity and interest in science lessons for 11-14 year olds; the "Improving Science and Emotional Development" project. *International Journal of Science Education, 26*(3), 281–308.

Matthews, B. (2005). *Engaging Education: Developing Emotional Literacy*. Maidenhead: Open University Press.

McCrone, J. (1992). *The Ape that Spoke: Language and the Evolution of the Human Mind* (3rd ed.). New York: Avon Books.

McLaren, P. & Kincheloe, J. L. (Eds.). (2007). *Critical Pedagogy: Where are We Now?* New York: Peter Lang Publishers.

Minstrell, J. (2000). Implications for teaching and learning inquiry: A summary. In J. Minstrell & E. H. van Zee (Eds.), *Inquiring into Inquiry Learning and Teaching in Science* (pp. 471–496). Washington, DC: American Association for the Advancement of Science (AAAS).

Minstrell, J. & van Zee, E. H. (Eds.). (2000). *Inquiring into Inquiry Learning and Teaching in Science*. Washington, DC: American Association for the Advancement of Science (AAAS).

Moore, A. H., Fowler, S. B., Jesiek, B. K., Moore, J. F., & Watson, C. E. (2008). *Learners 2.0? IT and 21st Century Learners in Higher Education*. Retrieved from http://net.educause.edu/ir/library/pdf/ERB0807.pdf

Moscovici, H. (1994, Spring). *An Interpretive Investigation of Teaching and Learning in a College Biology Course for Prospective Elementary and Early Childhood Teachers*. Unpublished doctoral dissertation, The Florida State University, Tallahassee, FL.

Moscovici, H. (2002a). Dynamics of power in teaching college biology: Influence on students' learning. In P. C. S. Taylor, P. J. Gilmer, & K. Tobin (Eds.), *Transforming Undergraduate Science Teaching: Social Constructivist Perspectives* (pp. 91–116). University of Pennsylvania: Lang Publishers.

Moscovici, H. (2002b). Task dynamics in a college biology course for prospective elementary teachers. *School Science and Mathematics, 101*(7), 372–379.

Moscovici, H. (2003a). The way I see it: Resisting teacher control or getting immersed in learning. *Journal of Research in Science Teaching, 40*(1), 98–100.

Moscovici, H. (2003b). Secondary science emergency permit teachers' perspective on power relations in their environments and the effects of these powers on classroom practices. *Teacher Education Quarterly, 30*(2), 41–54.

Moscovici, H. (2007). Mirror, mirrors on the wall, who is the most powerful of all? A self-analysis of power relationships in science methods courses. *Journal of Research in Science Teaching, 44*(9), 1370–1388.

Moscovici, H. (2009). Science teacher retention in today's urban schools: A study of success and failure. *Urban Education, 44*(1), 88–105.

Moscovici, H., & Gilmer, P. J. (1996). Testing alternative assessment strategies - The ups and downs for science-teaching faculty. *Journal for College Science Teaching, 25*(5), 319–323.

Moscovici, H., & Osisioma, I. (2009). Resolving issues of cultural discontinuity on co-facilitation of professional development activities. In K. C. Wieseman & M. H. Weinburgh (Eds.), *Women's Experiences in Leadership in k-16 Science Education Communities: Becoming and Being* (pp. 81–94). New York: Springer.

Moscovici, H., & Varrella, G. F. (2007). International professional development as a form of globalisation. In W. Atweh, A. Calabrese-Barton, M. Borba, N. Gough, C. Keitel, C. Vistro-Yu, et al. (Eds.), *Internationalisation and Globalisation in Mathematics and Science Education* (pp. 285–302). Dordrecht: The Netherlands: Springer.

National Council of Teachers of Mathematics (NCTM). (2000). *Principles and Standards for School Mathematics*. Reston, VA: Author.

National Council of Teachers of Mathematics (NCTM). (2011). Retrieved from http://www.nctm.org/standards/content.aspx?id=26798

National Geographic. (2011). *Brain*. Retrieved from http://science.nationalgeographic.com/science/health-and-human-body/human-body/brain-article.html

National Research Council (NRC). (1996). *National Science Education Standards*. Washington, DC: National Academy Press.

National Research Council (NRC). (2000). *Inquiry and the National Science Education Standards*. Washington, DC: National Academy Press.

National Research Council (NRC). (2001). *Adding It Up: Helping Children Learn Mathematics*. Washington, DC: National Academy Press.

National Research Council (NRC). (2005). *How Students Learn: History, Mathematics, and Science in the Classroom*. Washington, DC: National Academies of Science. Retrieved from http://www.nap.edu/catalog/10126.html

National Research Council (NRC). (2011). *A Framework for K-12 Science Education: Practices, Crosscutting Concepts, and Core Ideas*. Retrieved from http://www.nap.edu/catalog.php?record_id=13165

National Science Teachers Association (NSTA). (2011, June). *Quality Science Education and 21st-century Skills: Position Statement*. Retrieved from http://www.nsta.org/about/positions/21stcentury.aspx?lid=exp&print=true

Nevid, J. S., Rathus, S. A., & Greene, B. (2003). *Abnormal Psychology in a Changing World* (5th ed.). Upper Saddle River, NJ: Pearson-Prentice Hall.

Noddings, N. (1984). *Caring, A Feminine Approach to Ethics and Moral Education*. Berkeley, CA: University of California Press.

Oatley, K., & Johnson-Laird, P. N. (1987). Towards a cognitive theory of emotions. *Cognition and Emotion, 1*, 29–50.

Oltmanns, E. F., & Emery, R. E. (2003). *Abnormal Psychology* (4th ed.). Upper Saddle River, NJ: Pearson-Prentice Hall.

O'Neall, D. (2010). *Early Modern Homo Sapiens*. Retrieved from http://anthro.palomar.edu/homo2/mod_homo_4.htm

Orloff, J. (2005). *Positive Energy: 10 Extraordinary Prescriptions for Transforming Fatigue, Stress & Fear into Vibrance, Strength & Love*. New York: Three Rivers Press.

Ortony, A., & Turner, T. J. (1990). What's basic about basic emotions? *Psychological Review, 97*, 315–331.

Perez, M., Anand, P., Speroni, C., Parrish, T., Esra, P., Socias, M., et al. (2007). *Successful California Schools in the Context of Educational Adequacy*. Stanford, CA: American Institutes for Research. Retrieved from http://irepp.stanford.edu/documents/GDF/STUDIES/17-AIR-Successful-Schools/17-Successful-California-Schools(3-07).pdf

Ramsey-Gessert, L., & Shroyer, G. M. (1992). Enhancing science teaching self-efficacy in pre-service elementary teachers. *Journal of Elementary Science Education, 4*(1), 26–34.

Reeves, D. B. (2005). *High Performance in High Poverty Schools: 90/90/90 and Beyond*. Newark, DE: International Reading Association. Retrieved from http://www.sjboces.org/nisl/high%20performance%2090%2090%2090%20and%20beyond.pdf

Rennie, L. J., & Punch, K. F. (1991). The relationship between affect and achievement in science. *Journal of Research in Science Teaching, 28*, 193–209.

Ritchie, S. M., Tobin, K., Hudson, P., Roth, W-M, & Mergard, V. (2011). Reproducing successful rituals in bad times: Exploring emotional interactions of a new science teacher. *Science Education, 95*, 745–765.

Rodriguez, A. J. (1998). Strategies for counterresistance: Toward sociotransformative constructivism and learning to teach science for diversity and for understanding. *Journal of Research in Science Teaching, 35*, 589–622.

Rogoff, B. & Lave, J. (Eds.). (1984). *Everyday Cognition: Its Development in Social Context.* Cambridge, MA: Harvard University Press.

Roth, W.-M., Ritchie, S. M., Hudson, P., & Mergard, V. (2011). A study of laughter in science lessons. *Journal of Research in Science Teaching, 48*(5), 437–458.

Ryan, J. (1989). Study skills for the sciences: A bridge over troubled water. *Journal of College Science Teaching, 18*(6), 373–377.

Salovey, P., Detweiler-Bedell, B. T., Detweiler-Bedell, J. B., & Mayer, J. D. (2008). Emotional intelligence. In M. Lewis, J. M. Haviland-Jones, & L. F. Barrett (Eds.), *Handbook of Emotions* (3rd ed., pp. 533–547). New York: The Guilford Press.

Sarason, S. B. (2004). *And What Do You Mean by Learning?* Portsmouth, NH: Heinemann.

Schibeci R. A., & Riley J. P. (1986). Influence of students' background and perceptions on science attitudes and achievement. *Journal of Research in Science Teaching, 23*, 177–187.

Schnoop, J. (2008). *Judging Nine TV Judges.* Retrieved from http://www.aoltv.com/2008/01/31/judging-nine-tv-judges/

Schoenfeld, A. H. (2003). How can we examine the connections between teachers' world views and their educational practices? *Issues in Education, 8*(2), 217–227.

Schoenfeld, A. H. (2004). The math wars. *Educational Policy, 18*(1), 253–286.

Seyfarth, J. (2008). *Human Resource Leadership for Effective Schools* (5th ed.). Boston: Pearson Education, Inc.

Shulman, L. S. (1986). Those who understand: Knowledge growth in teaching. *Educational Researcher, 15*(2), 4–14.

Simpson, R. D., & Oliver, J. S. (1990). A summary of major influences on attitude toward achievement in science among adolescent students. *Science Education, 74*, 1–18.

Singer, F. M. (2007). Balancing globalization and local identity in the reform in education in Romania. In W. Atweh, A. Calabrese-Barton, M. Borba, N. Gough, C. Keitel, C. Vistro-Yu, et al. (Eds.), *Internationalisation and Globalisation in Mathematics and Science Education* (pp. 365–382). Dordrecht: The Netherlands: Springer.

Singer, F. M., & Moscovici, H. (2008). Teaching and learning cycles in a constructivist approach to instruction. *Teaching and Teacher Education, 24*(6), 1613–1634.

Siry, C. (2009). Expanding the field of science education: A conversation with Ken Tobin. *Eurasia Journal of Mathematics, Science & Technology Education, 5*(3), 197–207. Retrieved from http://www.ejmste.com/v5n3/EURASIA_v5n3_Siry.pdf

Smith, F. (2002). *The Glass Wall: Why Mathematics can Seem Difficult?* New York: Teachers College Press.

Smithsonian National Museum of Natural History. (2010). *What Does It Mean to be Human?* Retrieved from http://humanorigins.si.edu/evidence/human-fossils/species/homo-sapiens

Society for Neuroscience. (2005, February). *Phobia. Brain Briefings.* Retrieved from http://www.sfn.org/skins/main/pdf/BrainBriefings/BrainBriefings_Feb2005.pdf

Society for Neuroscience. (2005, December). *Love and the Brain.* Retrieved from http://www.sfn.org/skins/main/pdf/BrainBriefings/BrainBriefings_Dec2005.pdf

Society for Neuroscience. (2008). *Brain Facts: A Primer on the Brain and Nervous System.* Washington, DC: Author.

Stein, M. K., Smith, M. S., & Silver, E. A. (1999). The development of professional developers: Learning to assist teachers in new settings in new ways. *Harvard Educational Review, 69*(3), 237–270.

Sylwester, R. (1994). *How Emotions Affect Learning. Educational Leadership.* Retrieved from http://clint.sharedwing.net/research/clarissa/how%20emotions%20affect%20learning.pdf

Taylor, P. (1996). Mythmaking and mythbreaking in the mathematics classroom. *Educational Studies in Mathematics, 31*, 151–173.

Tchudi, S., & Lafer, S. (1996). *The Interdisciplinary Teacher's Handbook: Integrating Teaching across the Curriculum*. Portsmouth, NH: Heinemann.

The Evergreen State College. (2010). *Evaluation Process at Evergreen*. Retrieved from http://www.evergreen.edu/evaluations/

The Partnership for the 21st Century Skills. (2006). *Results that Matter: 21st Century Skills and High School Reform*. Retrieved from http://www.p21.org/index.php?option=com_content&task=view&id=204&Itemid=114

The Partnership for the 21st Century Skills. (2009). *The MILE Guide: Milestones for Improving Learning and Education*. Retrieved from http://www.p21.org/documents/MILE_Guide_091101.pdf

Tobias, S. (1980). *Overcoming Math Anxiety*. Boston: Houghton Mifflin Company.

Tobias, S. (1987). *Succeed with Math: Every Student's Guide to Conquering Math Anxiety*. New York: College Entrance Examination Board.

Tobias, S. (1990). *They're Not Dumb, They're Different. Stalking the Second Tear*. Tucson, AZ: Research Corporation.

Tobias, S. (1992). *Revitalizing Undergraduate Science: Why Some Things Work and Most Don't*. Tucson, AZ: Research Corporation.

Tobias, S., & Tomizuka, C. T. (1992). *Breaking the Science Barrier: How to Explore and Understand the Sciences*. New York: College Entrance Examination Board.

Tobin, K. G. (1991). *Constructivist Perspectives on Learning Environments*. Paper presented at the annual meeting of the American Educational Research Association, Chicago, IL.

Tobin, K. G. (1993a). Referents for making sense of science teaching. *International Journal of Science Education, 15*(3), 241–254.

Tobin, K. (1993b, April). *Learning as an Interactive Process in Social Settings*. Paper presented at the annual meeting of the American Educational Research Association, Atlanta, GA.

Tsui, J. M., & Mazzocco, M. M. M. (2007). *Effects of Math Anxiety and Perfectionism on Timed versus Untimed Math Testing in Mathematically Gifted Sixth Graders*. Retrieved from http://msdp.kennedykrieger.org/pdf/34.pdf

Turner, J. H. (2002). *Face to Face: Toward a Theory of Interpersonal Behavior*. Stanford, CA: Stanford University Press.

Turner, T. J., & Ortony, A. (1992). Basic emotions: Can conflicting criteria converge? *Psychological Review, 99*(3), 566–571. Retrieved from http://www.csun.edu/~gk45683/Turner%20and%20Ortony%20(1992).pdf

Turner, J. H., & Stets, J. E. (2006). Sociological theories of human emotions. *Annual Review of Sociology, 32*, 25–52. Retrieved from http://www.unc.edu/~nielsen/special/s7/sample_ARS_1col_2006.pdf

U.S. 107th Congress. (2002). *No Child Left Behind Act of 2001*. Retrieved from http://www2.ed.gov/policy/elsec/leg/esea02/107-110.pdf

van de Walle, J. (2004). *Elementary and Middle School Mathematics: Teaching Developmentally* (5th ed.). Boston: Pearson Education, Inc.

Van Sickle, M., & Cudahy, D. (2009). Laying the ladder down: Egalitarian leadership. In K. C. Wieseman & M. H. Weinburgh (Eds.), *Women's Experiences in Leadership in K-16 Science Education Communities: Becoming and Being* (pp. 155–166). New York: Springer.

Vergano, D. (2006). *Study: Emotion Rules the Brain's Decisions*. Retrieved from http://www.usatoday.com/tech/science/discoveries/2006-08-06-brain-study_x.htm

Vidal, C. (2008). *What is a Worldview?* Retrieved from http://cogprints.org/6094/2/Vidal_2008%2Dwhat%2Dis%2Da%2Dworldview.pdf

Vygotsky, L. S. (1978). *Mind in Society: The Development of Higher Psychological Processes*. Cambridge, MA: Harvard University Press.

WebChron: The Web Chronology Project. (2010). *China and East Asia Chronology: Lao-Tse b. 604 BC*. Retrieved from http://www.thenagain.info/webchron/china/LaoTse.html

Wertsch, J. V. (1985). *Vygotsky and the Social Formation of Mind*. Cambridge, MA: Harvard University Press.

Whitehead, A. N. (1967). *The Aims of Education and Other Essays.* New York: Free Press.

Wieseman, K. C., & Weinburgh, M. (Eds.). (2009). *Women's Experiences in Leadership in K-16 Science Education Communities: Becoming and Being.* New York: Springer.

Wieseman, K. C., Weinburgh, M., Moscovici, H., Fraser-Abder, P., Spector, B., Lew, L-Y., et al. (2005a, January). *Balancing Academic/professional and Personal Lives: Women's Experiences in Science Education.* Round table discussion presented at International meeting of the Association for the Educators of Teachers in Science, Colorado Springs, CO.

Wieseman, K. C., Yeotis, C., Weinburgh, M., Moscovici, H., Koch, J., Fraser-Abder, P., et al. (2005b, April). *Crucial Intersections in Academic/Professional and Personal Lives: Women's Experiences in Science Education.* Special colloquium presented at the annual meeting of the National Association for Research in Science Teaching, Dallas, TX.

Wiggins, G., & McTighe, J. (1998). *Understanding by Design.* Alexandria, VA: Association for Supervision and Curriculum Development (ASCD).

Wikipedia. (2010). *World View.* Retrieved from http://en.wikipedia.org/wiki/World_view

Wikipedia. (2011, February). *Functional Magnetic Resonance Imaging.* Retrieved from http://en.wikipedia.org/wiki/Functional_magnetic_resonance_imaging

Wikipedia. (2011, March). *Chemical Basis of Love.* Retrieved from http://en.wikipedia.org/wiki/Chemical_basis_for_love

Wikipedia. (2011, March 8). *Dopamine.* Retrieved form http://en.wikipedia.org/wiki/Dopamine

Wikipedia. (2011, March 15). *Endorphin.* Retrieved from http://en.wikipedia.org/wiki/Endorphin

Willson, V. L. (1983). A meta-analysis of the relationship between science achievement and science attitude. *Journal of Research in Science Teaching, 12,* 31–39.

Winerman, L. (2006). Talking the pain away. *Monitor on Psychology, 37*(9), 35. Retrieved from http://www.apa.org/monitor/oct06/talking.html

Yeh, S. S. (2001). Tests worth teaching to: Constructing state-mandated tests that emphasize critical thinking. *Educational Researcher, 30*(9), 12–17.

Yukl, G. A. (1989). *Leadership in Organizations* (2nd ed.). Englewood Cliffs, NJ: Prentice Hall.

Yukl, G. (2006). *Leadership in Organizations* (6th ed.). Upper Saddle River, NJ: Pearson/Prentice Hall.

Zoller, U. (2001). Alternative assessment as critical means of facilitating HOCS-promoting teaching and learning in chemistry education. *Chemical Education: Research and Practice in Europe, 2*(1), 9–17. Retrieved from http://www.uoi.gr/cerp/2001_February/pdf/04Zoller.pdf

INDEX

Printed in the United States
By Bookmasters